Copyright © 2011 by PAGODA Books

All rights reserved. No part of this publication may be reproduced, stored in a retrieval system, or transmitted, in any form, or by any means, electronic, mechanical, photocopying, recording or otherwise, without the prior written permission of the copyright holder and the publisher.

Published by PAGODA Books
PAGODA Books is the professional language publishing company of the PAGODA Education Group.
PAGODA Tower 1306-6, 7, Seocho-Dong,
Seocho-Gu, Seoul, Korea 137-855
www.pagodabook.com

1st Published 2011
26th impression 2025
Printed in the Republic of Korea

ISBN 978-89-6281-245-9 (14740)

Publisher | Seo-Jin Park
Writers | PAGODA Language Education Center

Acknowledgements
Thanks to the following for their contributions in providing us feedback:
Ahmi Cha, Rachel Shin, Joanne Lee, Sooji Park, Josephine Kim, Ella Kim, Kay Lim, Elisa Lee, Daniel Lee, Hanna Lee, Rose Shin, Mia Kim, Sue Ahn, Christina Lee

A defective book may be exchanged at the store where you purchased it.

Introduction

i Can Speak 2 Red, the second level of the *i* Can Speak series, is a speaking-focused course book for English learners who are at a pre-intermediate level. This book gives learners the opportunity to practice useful expressions in various authentic situations. This book also combines speaking and listening activities that students can actively participate in during pair work or group work.

There are 16 lessons in this book and each lesson consists of the following sections:

Warm-Up

This section helps learners brainstorm the topic of the lesson and brings up some casual questions to talk about.

Dialogue

This section covers target sentences in authentic conversations between two or three people. It also improves listening skills and creates interest because the dialogue mirrors everyday spoken English.

Language Focus

This section provides some key expressions in different situations for each lesson and contains an overview of the sentence structures. This provides learners with a quick reference while doing the exercises.

Pronunciation

This section provides learners with key pronunciation exercises that are chosen from the dialogue. These exercises contain continuous practicing of sounds to help non-native speakers to pronounce words like native speakers.

Talk 1, 2

Each lesson includes two Talk sections. These sections provide warm-up questions with practice drills that make use of the new dialogues using the given words or expressions.

i Speak

This section offers speaking activities that encourage learners to use the information from the lesson to ask and answer questions with their peers. It aims to build learners' confidence and interest in communicative situations.

i Speak & Listen

This section contains both listening and speaking activities. Learners are to listen to the dialogues in the audio and use these skills as they engage in the next speaking activities. The activities allow learners to check their understanding of each lesson and also serve as a way to wrap up the lesson.

*This course book is used best in collaboration with the on-line program.

Scope and Sequence

Introduction ——————— 3   **Classroom Language** ——————— 6-7

	Topic	**Functions**	**Page**
Lesson 1 It's a pleasure to meet you.	Greetings	Making introductions and greeting people	8
Lesson 2 Do you like your job?	Jobs	Talking about occupations	14
Lesson 3 What time is the party?	Times and Days of Events	Talking about plans (times, days, and dates)	20
Lesson 4 What's the weather like in Rome?	Weather and Temperature	Talking about weather conditions and temperature around the world	26
Lesson 5 Which season do you like the best?	Seasonal Activities	Talking about favorite seasons and seasonal activities	32
Lesson 6 How many people are there in your family?	Family	Talking about family members and birth order	38
Lesson 7 Who do you take after?	Resemblance	Talking about family resemblance	44
Lesson 8 What's he like?	Personality	Describing people's personality types	50

	Topic	Functions	Page
Lesson 9 **Do you ever use dental floss?**	Health Habits	Discussing health and frequency of activities	56
Lesson 10 **What does it look like?**	Descriptions	Describing things and their uses	62
Lesson 11 **It should be on the coffee table.**	Locations	Describing locations of objects	68
Lesson 12 **Is there a flower shop around here?**	Places	Giving directions	74
Lesson 13 **Do you like musicals?**	Likes and Dislikes I	Talking about likes and dislikes	80
Lesson 14 **What kinds of movies do you like?**	Likes and Dislikes II	Talking about likes and dislikes (Wh-Questions)	86
Lesson 15 **I'm looking for a minidress.**	Shopping	Interacting with salespeople	92
Lesson 16 **What's today's special?**	Restaurant	Placing orders and making complaints	98

Classroom Language

Teacher's Talk

Students' Talk

Lesson 1
It's a pleasure to meet you.

Warm-Up Do you like meeting new people?
Do you like introducing people to your friends?

Dialogue Listen to the dialogue and practice.

Sarah: Hi, John! Long time no see.
John: Yes, it's been a long time. How have you been lately?
Sarah: Not bad. What about you?
John: Pretty good. Oh! Sarah, I'd like you to meet my co-worker, Robert. Robert, this is Sarah. She's my neighbor.
Robert: Nice to meet you, Sarah.
Sarah: It's a pleasure to meet you, too, Robert.
Robert: Where are you from?
Sarah: I'm from Korea. What about you?
Robert: I'm from the UK. Shall we have dinner together sometime?
Sarah: Sounds good to me.
Robert: Here's my business card. Give me a call when you're available.
Sarah: Sure.

Language Focus

Introductions

Kevin, **I'd like you to meet my friend**, Judy.
(= Kevin, **I'd like to introduce my friend**, Judy.)
Judy, **this is Kevin**. Kevin, **this is Judy**.

Nice to meet you.	Nice to meet you, too.
Glad to meet you.	Glad to meet you, too.
It's a pleasure to meet you.	It's a pleasure to meet you, too.

Greetings

How are you today / these days?	Great. / Pretty good.
How have you been lately?	Fine, thanks. / Not bad.
How's it going?	So-so. / Terrible.
What's up?	Nothing special. / Nothing new.
What are you up to?	

 **Pronunciation**   *Listen to the words and practice saying them.*

☐ **ee (/iː/)**

| see | meet | need | beef |
| keep | sheep | street | tree |

☐ **pr**

| pretty | pram | present | problem |
| prize | proud | print | pretty |

☐ **fr**

| friend | from | frame | frog |
| fresh | Friday | fruit | freedom |

Lesson 1 · 9

Talk 1

A Write the responses in the correct boxes.

> How's it going?

| Terrible. | Not bad. | Pretty good. | Not good. | OK. |
| Not so good, not so bad. | Fine. | Great. | So-so. | |

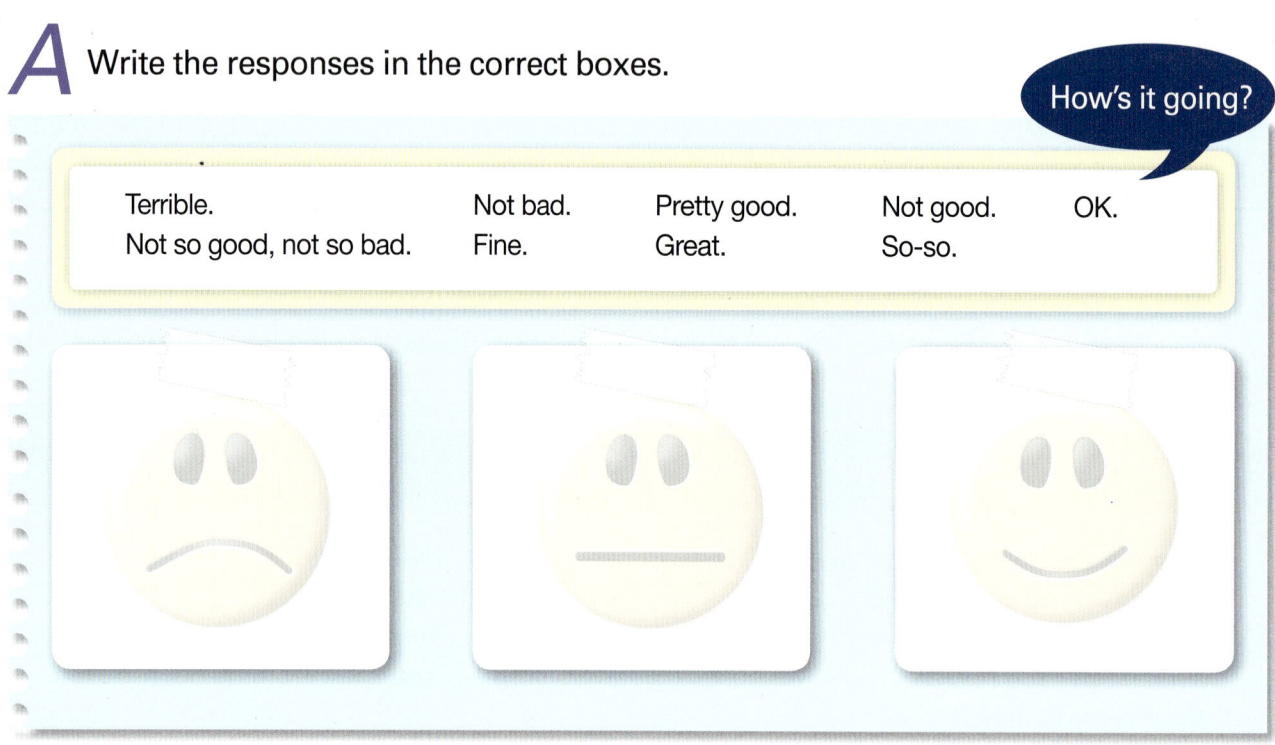

B Roleplay conversations with your partner, referring to the pictures.

Example

A: Hi, Jane. Good to see you again.
B: Good to see you, too, Chris. How's it going?
A: Pretty good. What about you?
B: Not bad.

Talk 2

A Complete the application for the social networking website, *Pal Club*, using the information in the box.

> thirtynine@example.com   Andrew   +1-640-869-4638
> Morgan   Canadian

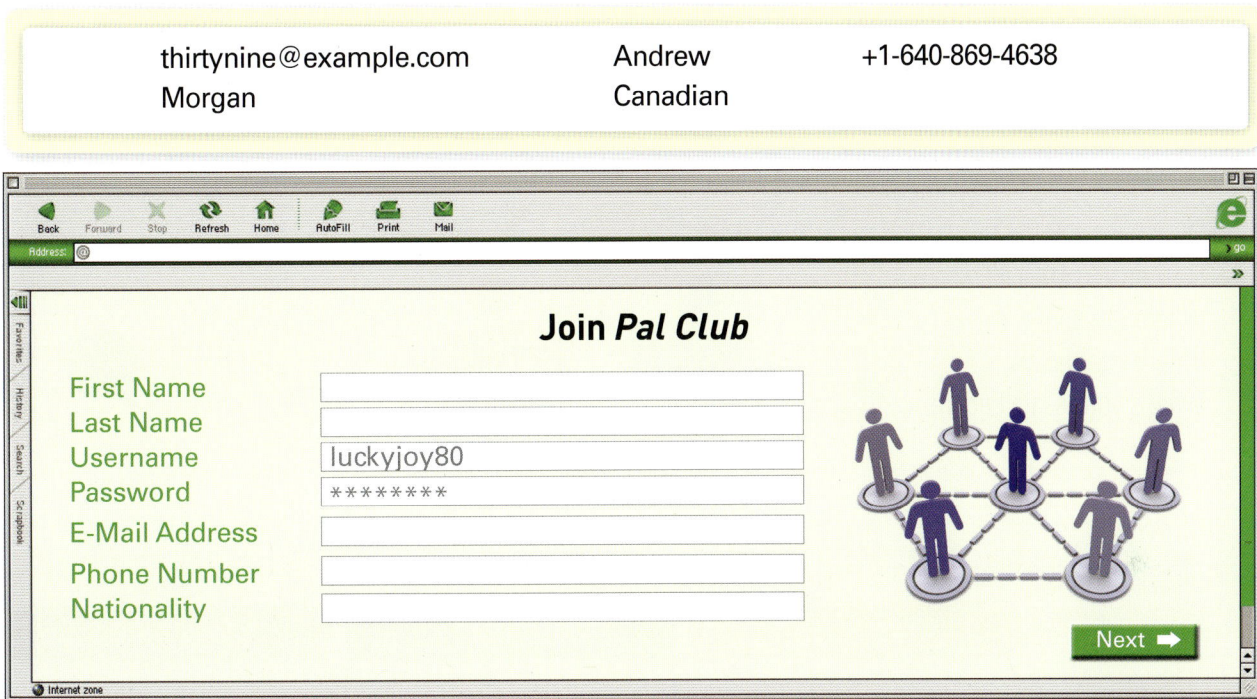

B Complete the application, using your own personal information. Then practice the dialogue with your partner.

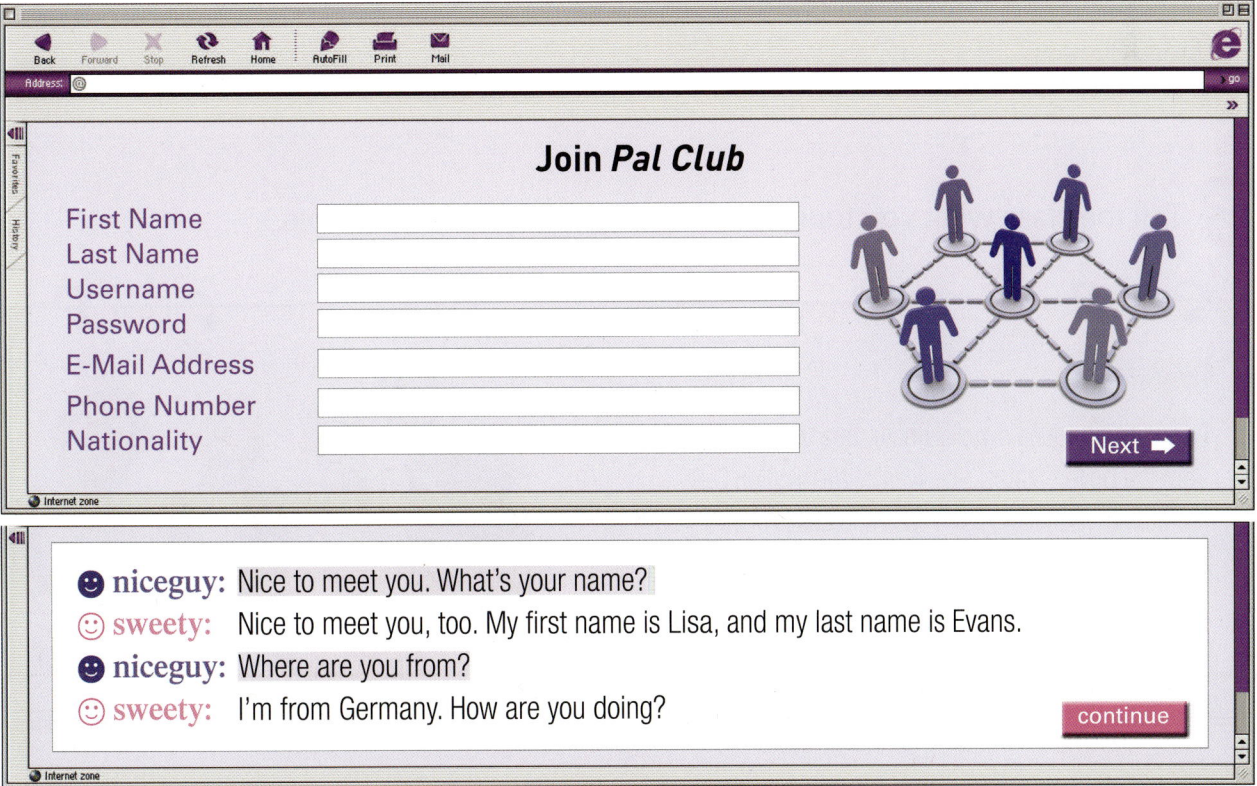

- **niceguy:** Nice to meet you. What's your name?
- **sweety:** Nice to meet you, too. My first name is Lisa, and my last name is Evans.
- **niceguy:** Where are you from?
- **sweety:** I'm from Germany. How are you doing?

i Speak

A Ask three classmates questions to complete the table.

Questions
May I ask you about yourself?
What's your name?
How do you spell it?
Where are you from?
Where do you live?
What's your e-mail address?

Answers
Sure. Go ahead.
My name is …
It's …
I'm from …
I live in …
It's … @……

@ = at

	Classmate 1	Classmate 2	Classmate 3
Name			
Country			
City			
E-Mail Address			

B Tell the class what you found out about one of your classmates.

Example

I'd like to introduce my classmate, Tara Jones. She is from the United States. She lives in Washington D.C. For more information, her e-mail address is daisy@google.com.

 **Speak & Listen**

A 🎧 Listen to the dialogues. Match the names with the pictures.

| Crystal | Eric | Danny | Ms Lee | Nate |

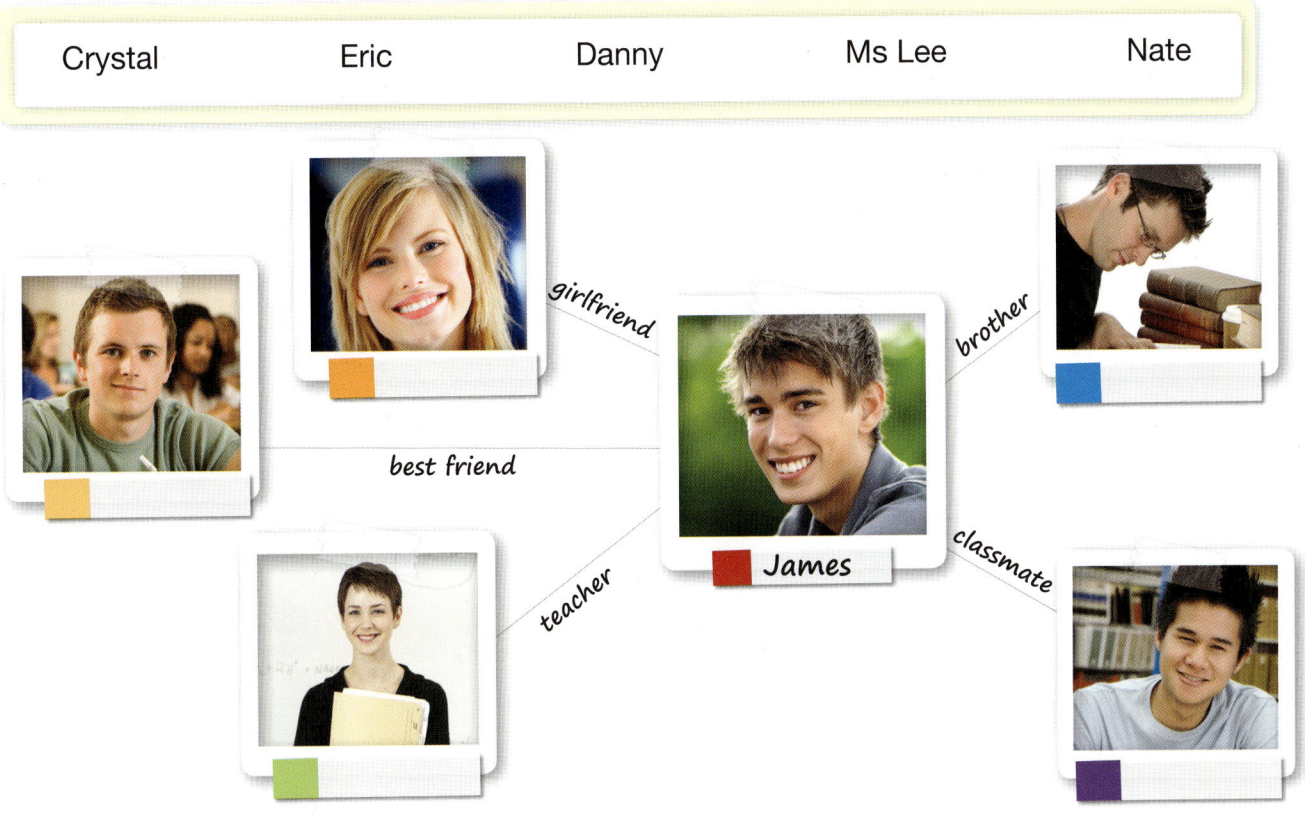

B Complete the diagram, using your own personal information. Then introduce the people to your partner.

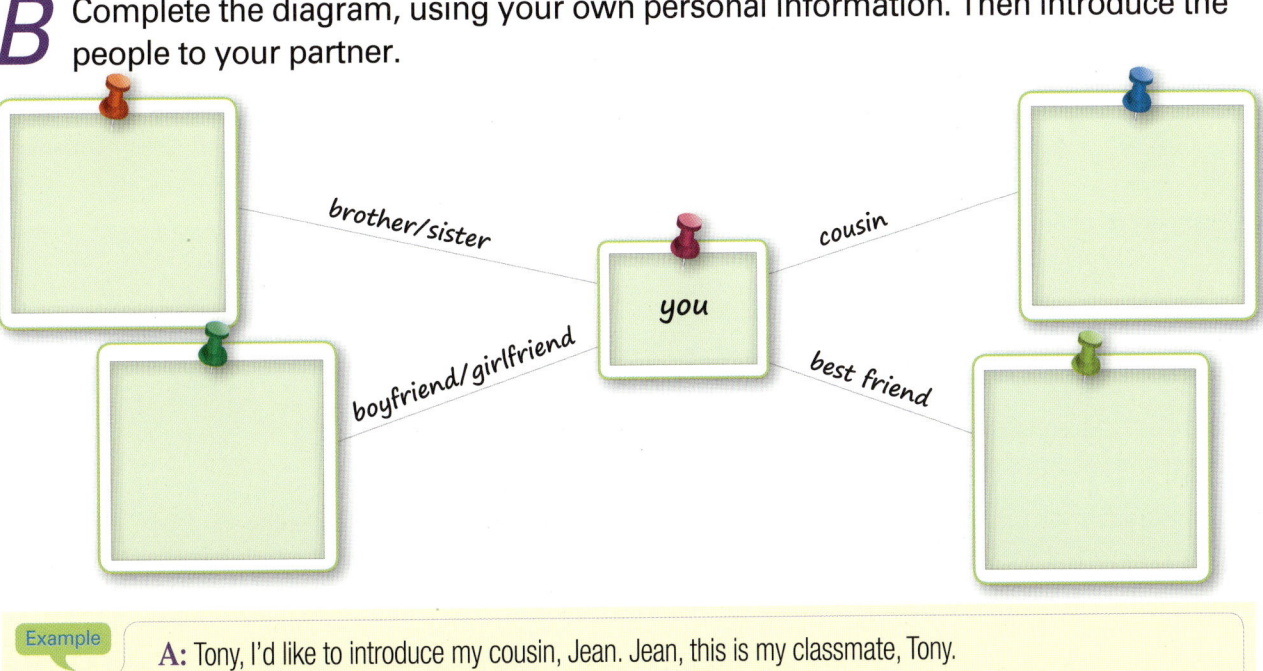

Example
A: Tony, I'd like to introduce my cousin, Jean. Jean, this is my classmate, Tony.
B: It's a pleasure to meet you, Jean. I've heard a lot about you.
C: It's a pleasure to meet you, Tony.

Lesson 2
Do you like your job?

Warm-Up What do you do for a living? What do you want to do in the future? In your opinion, what is the most stressful and challenging job?

Dialogue Listen to the dialogue and practice.

Chris: Emily, welcome to the party!
Emily: Thanks for inviting me. It seems like a nice party.
Chris: I hope you enjoy it. How are you these days?
Emily: Pretty good. How are you?
Chris: Not so bad.
Emily: It's good to hear that. What do you do for a living these days?
Chris: I'm a computer programmer.
Emily: That's a very challenging job, isn't it? Do you like your job?
Chris: It's a little bit stressful, but it's OK. You're a music teacher, right?
Emily: That's right.
Chris: How do you like your job?
Emily: Well, it's exciting.

Language Focus

Occupations	
What do you do?	I'm a graduate student.
What's your job/occupation?	I'm an interpreter.
What do you do for a living?	I'm a movie director.

Opinions about jobs	
Do you like your job?	Yes, I do. / No, I don't.
How do you like your job?	I like my job very much. I like my job at times. I don't like my job at all.
What do you think of your job?	It's **very interesting / exciting / relaxing**. It's **challenging/boring/tiring**.
Is your job stressful?	It's **not stressful at all / a little bit stressful / stressful / very stressful**.

Pronunciation

Listen to the words and practice saying them.

- ☐ **l**
little	like	left	leaf
late	lead	light	live

- ☐ **r**
right	rate	rain	river
ruler	read	rare	ride

- ☐ **ing**
living	going	jogging	hiking
swimming	challenging	gathering	inviting

Talk 1

A Match the job titles with the workplaces.

| bank | banker | fund manager | security guard |

| restaurant | hospital | publishing company |

| IT company | airline company | broadcasting company |

- news reporter, anchorperson, movie director
- banker, fund manager, security guard
- web designer, computer programmer, database consultant
- waiter/waitress, cashier, chef
- doctor, nurse, pharmacist
- flight attendant, pilot, check-in assistant
- editor, freelance writer, illustrator

B Roleplay conversations with your partner about the jobs in the pictures.

Example

A: What does he do?
B: He's a computer programmer.
A: Where does he work?
B: He works at an IT company.
A: Does he work part-time or full-time?
B: I think he works part-time.

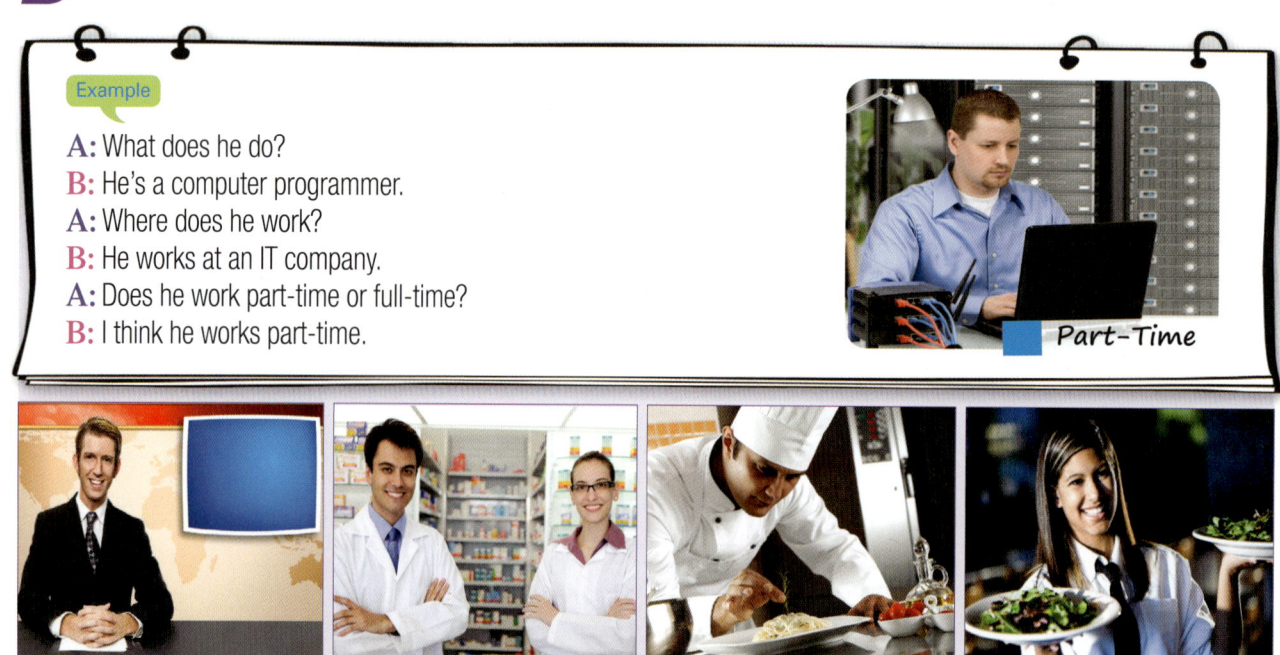

Full-Time Part-Time Full-Time Part-Time

Talk 2

A What do you think about each job? Write the adjectives under the pictures.

Firefighter

Librarian

News Reporter

Interpreter

Anchorperson

Veterinarian

Security Guard

Flight Attendant

exciting / interesting / relaxing → boring / tiring → challenging / dangerous

B Roleplay conversations with your partner, using the pictures below.

Example

A: What do you do for a living?
B: I'm a car salesperson.
A: Oh really? What do you think of your job?
B: Well, I think it's challenging in some ways.
A: Is it stressful?
B: Yes, it's a little stressful.

Car Salesperson

Stockbroker

Police Officer

Fashion Designer

Librarian

Lesson 2 · 17

i Speak

A Play the game below with your partner, using a coin. (Heads = move forward two spaces. Tails = move forward one space.) Make questions and answers, using the picture you land on. If the sentence is wrong, or if you can't make a sentence, move back one space. Whoever gets to the end first is the winner.

Example

A: What do you do?
A: Where do you work?
A: What do you think of your job?

B: I'm a cashier.
B: I work in a restaurant.
B: I think it's a little bit boring.

i Speak & Listen

A Listen to the dialogues. Match the names with the pictures.

ⓐ David ⓑ Vivian ⓒ Pamela
ⓓ Eric   ⓔ Cindy   ⓕ Brian

B Ask three classmates questions to complete the table below.

Name	Occupation	Workplace	Opinion About Job

Example

A: May I ask your name?
B: Sure. My name is Judy. J-U-D-Y.
A: Thanks. What do you do for a living?
B: I'm a doctor.
A: Oh, I see. Where do you work?
B: I work at the General Hospital.
A: How do you like your job?
B: Well, it's interesting, but it's a little bit stressful.
A: Thank you for participating.
B: Anytime.

Lesson 3
What time is the party?

Warm-Up Do you think you are a punctual person?
Do you keep a personal schedule?

Dialogue Listen to the dialogue and practice.

Liz: James, do you have the time? I forgot to bring my watch.
James: It's 5:20. Where are you going?
Liz: I'm going to my friend's birthday party. I'm a little late.
James: I see. What time is the party?
Liz: The party is at 5:30. Speaking of parties, are you going to Professor Alman's farewell party?
James: Oh, I didn't know about it. When is it?
Liz: It's on April 27th.
James: The 27th of April? What day is that? Is it a Friday?
Liz: No, it's a Thursday. Can you come?
James: Yes, I can. Fortunately, I'm free that day.
Liz: Great! Oh, I think the bus is coming.
James: OK. Enjoy the party and I'll see you on the 27th.

Language Focus

Times	
What time is it? Could you tell me the time? Do you have the time?	It's 3:00 (three o'clock). It's 5:30 (five-thirty) / It's half past five. It's 7:15 (seven-fifteen). / It's (a) quarter past seven. It's 8:45 (eight forty-five). / It's (a) quarter to nine. It's 2:50 (two-fifty). / It's ten to three.

Days and Dates	
What day is it today?	It's Tuesday.
What date is it today? What's the date today?	It's September 9th. / It's the 9th of September.
When is your birthday?	It's (on) February 23rd. / It's (on) the 23rd of February.

Pronunciation
Listen to the words and practice saying them.

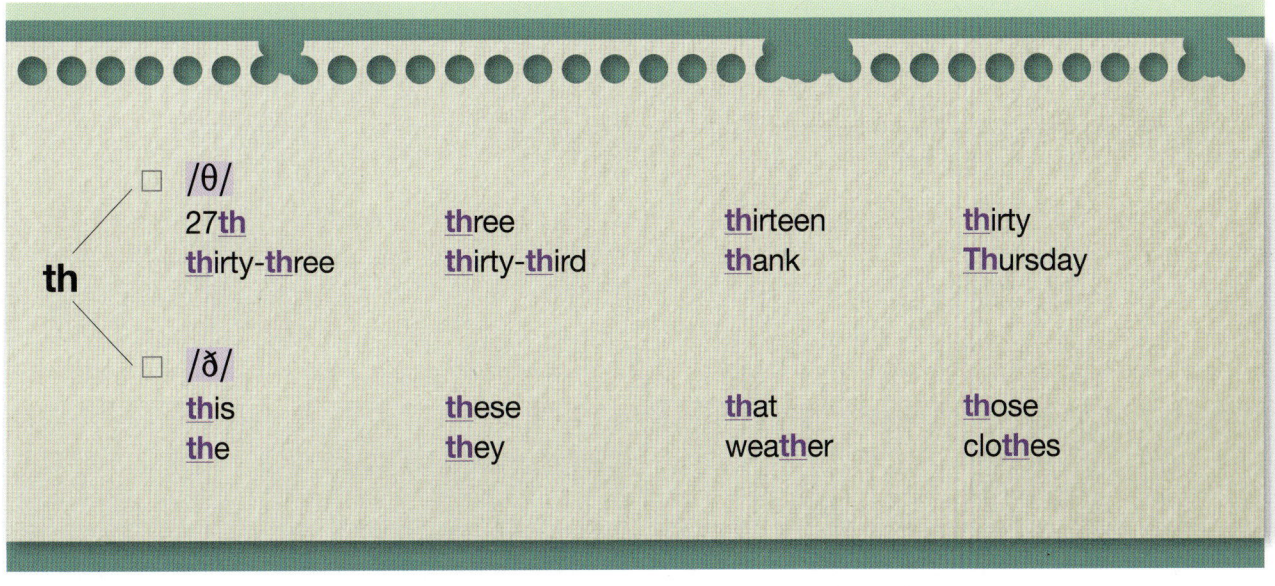

th

☐ /θ/
| 27th | three | thirteen | thirty |
| thirty-three | thirty-third | thank | Thursday |

☐ /ð/
| this | these | that | those |
| the | they | weather | clothes |

Talk 1

A Match the times.

It's **eight-thirty**.   •   [4:10]   •   • It's **ten to eleven**.

It's **ten-fifty**.   •   [6:45]   •   • It's **half past eight**.

It's **twelve-o-five**.   •   [12:05]   •   • It's **ten past four**.

It's **four-ten**.   •   [8:30]   •   • It's **a quarter to seven**.

It's **six-forty five**.   •   [2:15]   •   • It's **five past twelve**.

It's **two-fifteen**.   •   [10:50]   •   • It's **a quarter past two**.

B Roleplay conversations with a partner, using the information below.

> **Example**
> **A:** Excuse me, do you have the time?
> (= Could you tell me the time?)
> **B:** Yes. It's ten past seven.
> **A:** Oh no! I think I've missed the bus. Thanks, anyway.
> **B:** You're welcome.

7:10 BUS

12:15 Train

11:30 Plane

8:50 Express Bus

5:45 Ferry

i Can Speak **2 Red** 22

Talk 2

A Match the events with the pictures.

ⓐ wedding	ⓑ graduation	ⓒ birthday	ⓓ job interview
ⓔ final exam	ⓕ college reunion	ⓖ farewell party	ⓗ baby shower

B Roleplay conversations with a partner, referring to the calendars below.

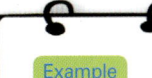
A: Anna's baby shower is coming up soon.
B: Really? When is the baby shower?
A: It's on the 5th of April.
B: What day is that?
A: It's a Friday.

i Speak

A Write three events on your calendar. Include times.

Month:						
Sun	Mon	Tue	Wed	Thurs	Fri	Sat
1	2	3	4	5	6	7
8	9	10	11	12	13	14
15	16	17	18	19	20	21
22	23	24	25	26	27	28
29	30	31				

B Referring to your canlendar above, talk with your partner about your plans.

 A: Do you have any special plans this month?
B: Well, I have my brother's wedding and my friend's baby shower.
A: Oh, really? When is the wedding?
B: It's (on) Thursday the 18th of July.
A: What time does it start?
B: (At) 3 pm.
A: I see. When is the baby shower?

 **Speak & Listen**

A 🎧 Listen to the dialogue. Check (✓) the events that are on Crystal's schedule for September.

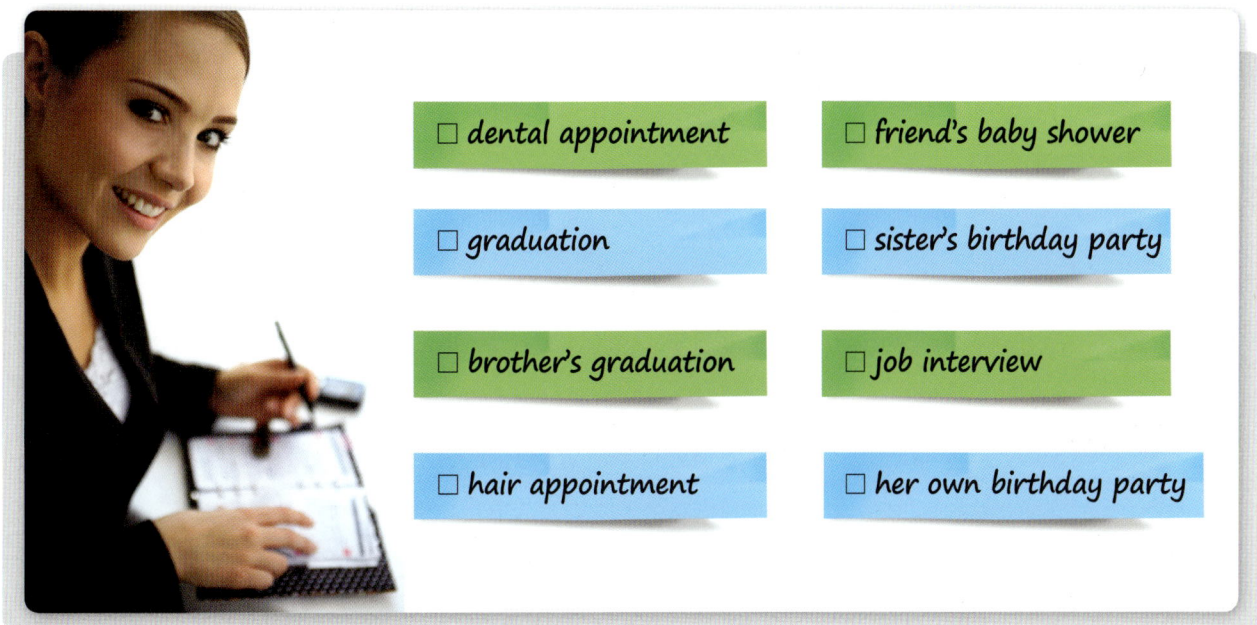

- ☐ dental appointment
- ☐ friend's baby shower
- ☐ graduation
- ☐ sister's birthday party
- ☐ brother's graduation
- ☐ job interview
- ☐ hair appointment
- ☐ her own birthday party

B 🎧 Listen to the dialogue again. Complete Crystal's diary for September. Then ask your partner questions to check your answers.

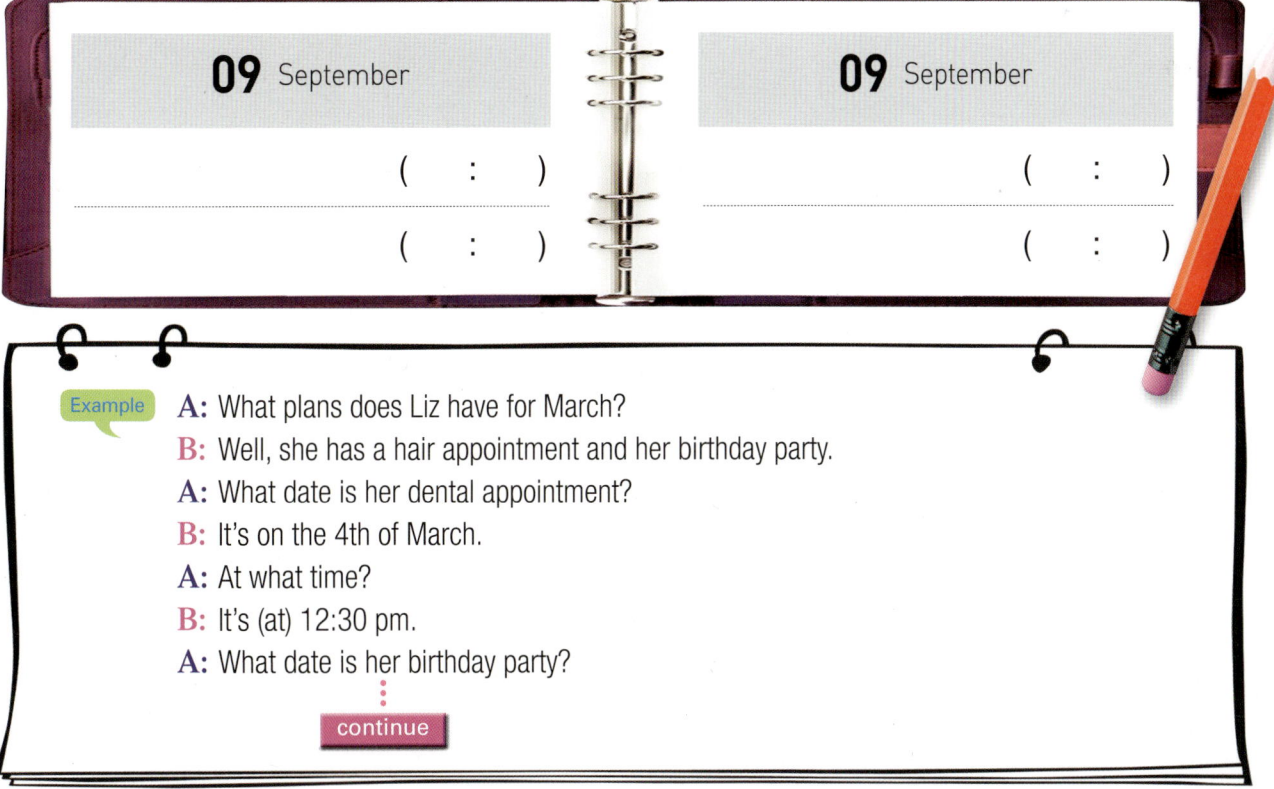

09 September   **09** September

(:)   (:)

(:)   (:)

Example
A: What plans does Liz have for March?
B: Well, she has a hair appointment and her birthday party.
A: What date is her dental appointment?
B: It's on the 4th of March.
A: At what time?
B: It's (at) 12:30 pm.
A: What date is her birthday party?
⋮
continue

Lesson 4: What's the weather like in Rome?

Warm-Up What's the weather like today?
Do you have friends or relatives overseas? If you do, where do they live? Find out what the weather is like there today.

Dialogue Listen to the dialogue and practice.

Sofia: Hello.
Jay: Hey, Sofia. This is Jay.
Sofia: Jay! I'm so glad you called. How are you doing in London?
Jay: I'm doing great so far. I made a lot of friends here.
Sofia: That sounds great.
Jay: Yes. But, the weather here is terrible.
Sofia: Why? How's the weather there?
Jay: Well, it's rainy and windy all day long. What's the weather like in Rome?
Sofia: It's sunny here.
Jay: Really? What's the temperature today?
Sofia: Today, it's 30°C.
Jay: Ah, lucky you! I want to go to Rome.
Sofia: Come and visit me anytime. The weather here is great!

Language Focus

Weather	
How's the weather today? What's the weather like in London?	It's clear/sunny/cloudy/foggy/ rainy/snowy/windy/stormy.
What kind of weather do you like? What's your favorite weather?	I like sunny days. My favorite weather is sunny weather.

Temperature	
What's the temperature?	It's 28°C (twenty-eight degrees Celsius). It's 84°F (eighty-four degrees Fahrenheit). It's -7°C (seven degrees below zero / minus 7 degrees).

Pronunciation — Listen to the words and practice saying them.

☐ **want to /wanna/**
I <u>want to</u> go to Rome.
I <u>want to</u> eat spaghetti in Italy.
Do you <u>want to</u> travel around Europe?
Does she <u>want to</u> live in France?

☐ **Silent d**
come <u>and</u> visit   go <u>and</u> see   on <u>and</u> off   eyes <u>and</u> nose

Talk 1

A Match the weather with the pictures.

| cloudy | rainy | sunny | snowy |
| windy | clear | stormy | foggy |

B Roleplay conversations with your partner about the weather and activities in the pictures.

Example

A: What kind of weather do you like?
B: I like cloudy days.
A: What do you like to do on a cloudy day?
B: I like to go shopping on a cloudy day. What about you?
A: Well, my favorite days are sunny days. I like to go on picnics on sunny days.

make a snowman | go windsurfing | go sunbathing | go driving | ride a bike | get some rest

Talk 2

A Write the items in the correct categories.

☀ Sunny	🌂 Rainy	🌬 Windy	⛄ Snowy

B Roleplay conversations with a partner, using the pictures below.

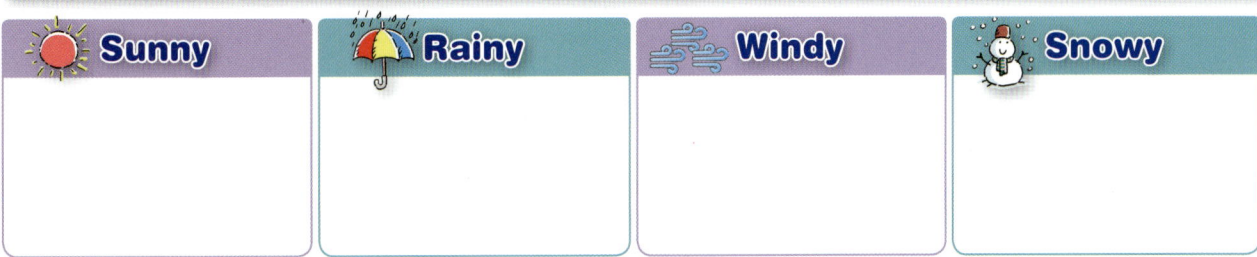

Example
A: How's the weather today?
B: It's sunny outside. You'd better wear a hat.
A: Oh, really? What's the temperature?
B: It's 23°C.

wear a hat — 23°C

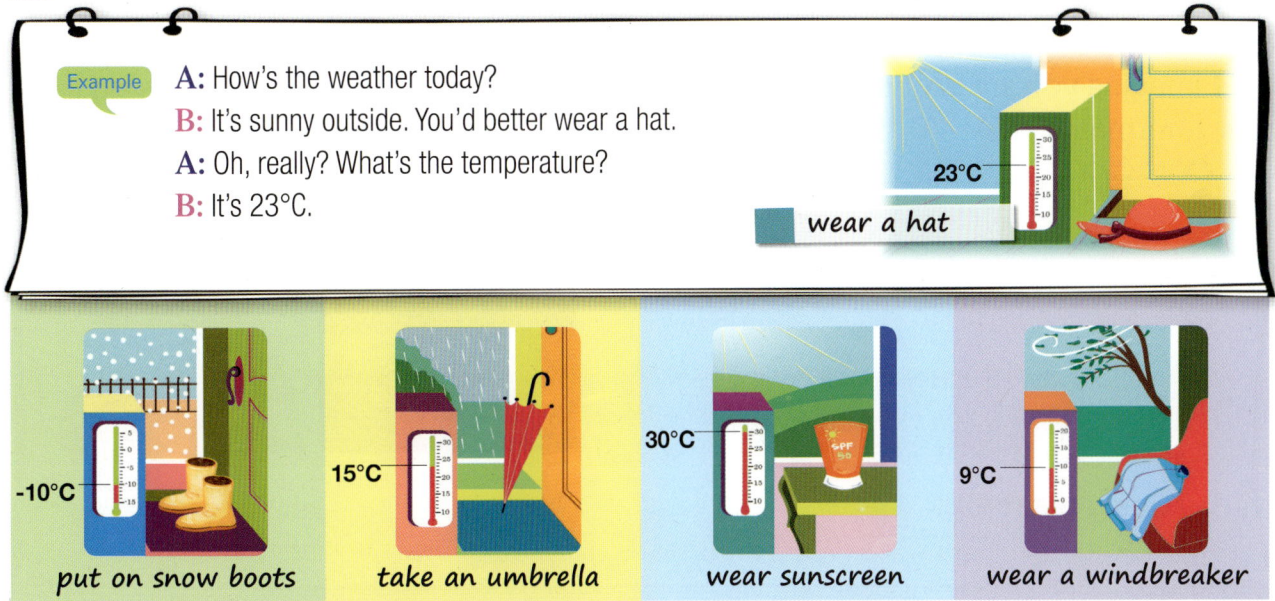

-10°C — put on snow boots
15°C — take an umbrella
30°C — wear sunscreen
9°C — wear a windbreaker

Lesson 4 · 29

i Speak

A Match the cities with the dots on the map.

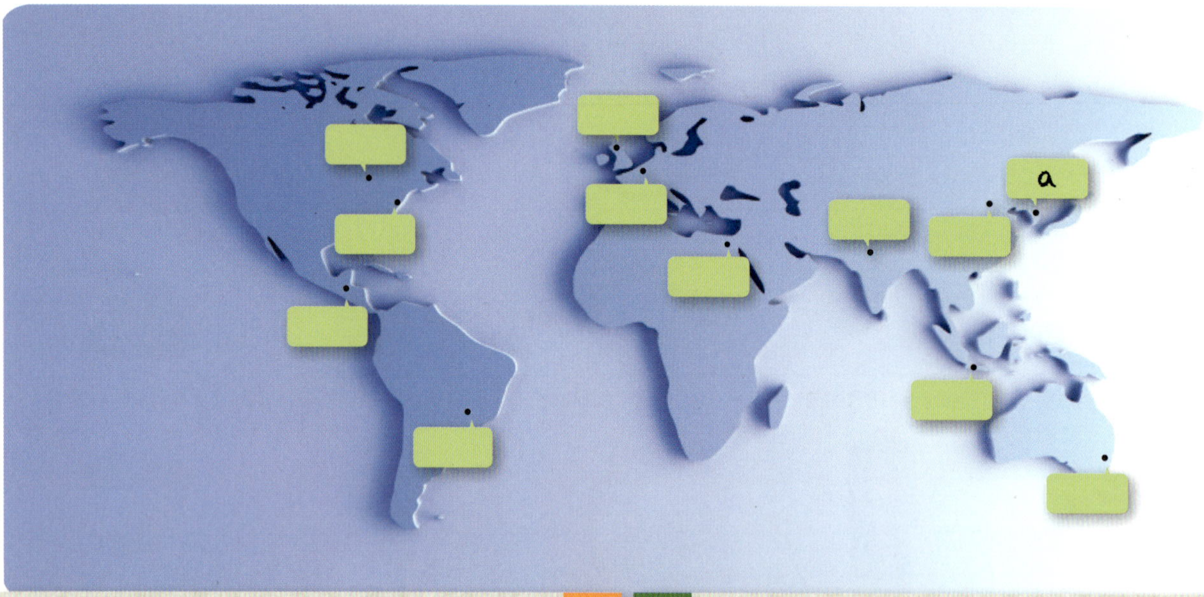

ⓐ Seoul		0°C		ⓖ Paris		4°C
ⓑ Beijing		-9°C		ⓗ Ottawa		-7°C
ⓒ Cairo		17°C		ⓘ Jakarta		30°C
ⓓ Washington D.C.		1°C		ⓙ Mexico City		15°C
ⓔ London		5°C		ⓚ Brasilia		23°C
ⓕ New Delhi		10°C		ⓛ Canberra		12°C

B Imagine you are in one of the cities shown in **A**. Roleplay conversations, using the information in **A**.

Example

A: Are you enjoying your world trip? Where are you now?
B: I'm in Beijing. What about you?
A: I'm in Cairo now. What's the weather like in Beijing?
B: It's snowy and -9°C. How's the weather in Cairo?
A: It's sunny and 30°C.
B: Hope you have a safe trip.
A: You too.

i Speak & Listen

A 🎧 Listen to the world weather report. Complete the table.

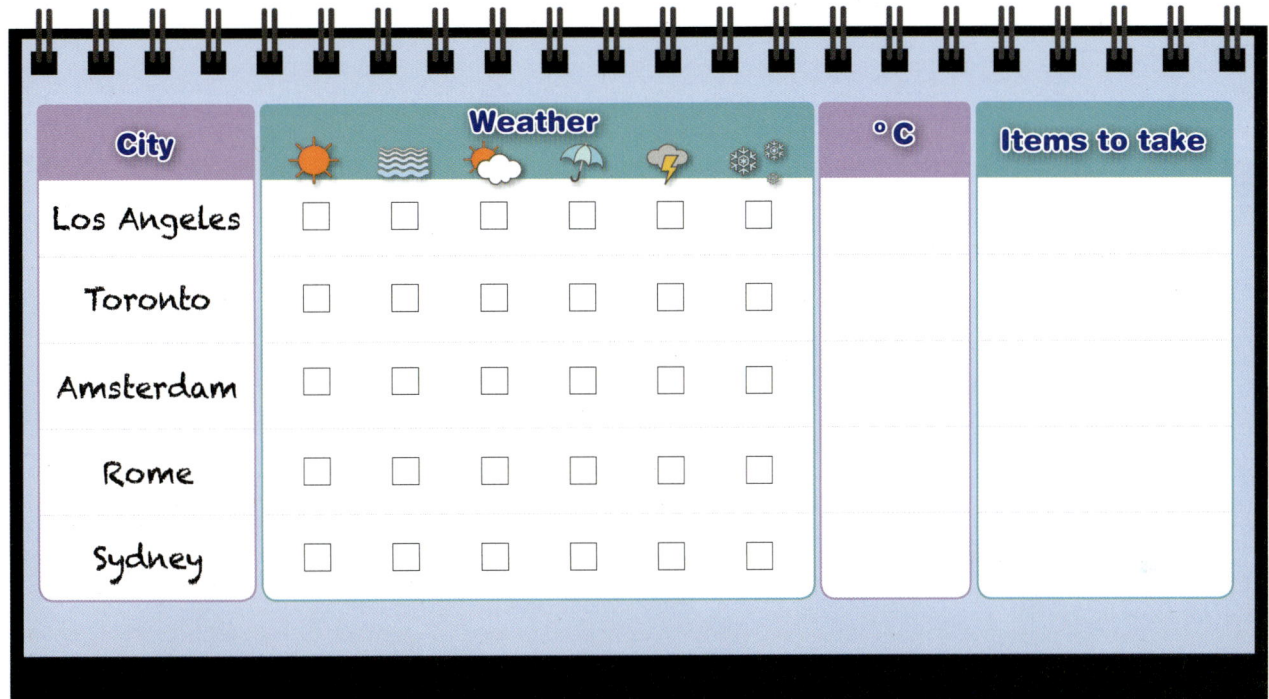

City	Weather ☀️	〰️	⛅	☂️	⚡	❄️	°C	Items to take
Los Angeles	☐	☐	☐	☐	☐	☐		
Toronto	☐	☐	☐	☐	☐	☐		
Amsterdam	☐	☐	☐	☐	☐	☐		
Rome	☐	☐	☐	☐	☐	☐		
Sydney	☐	☐	☐	☐	☐	☐		

B Imagine you are in one of the cities shown in **A**. Roleplay conversations, using the world weather report in **A**.

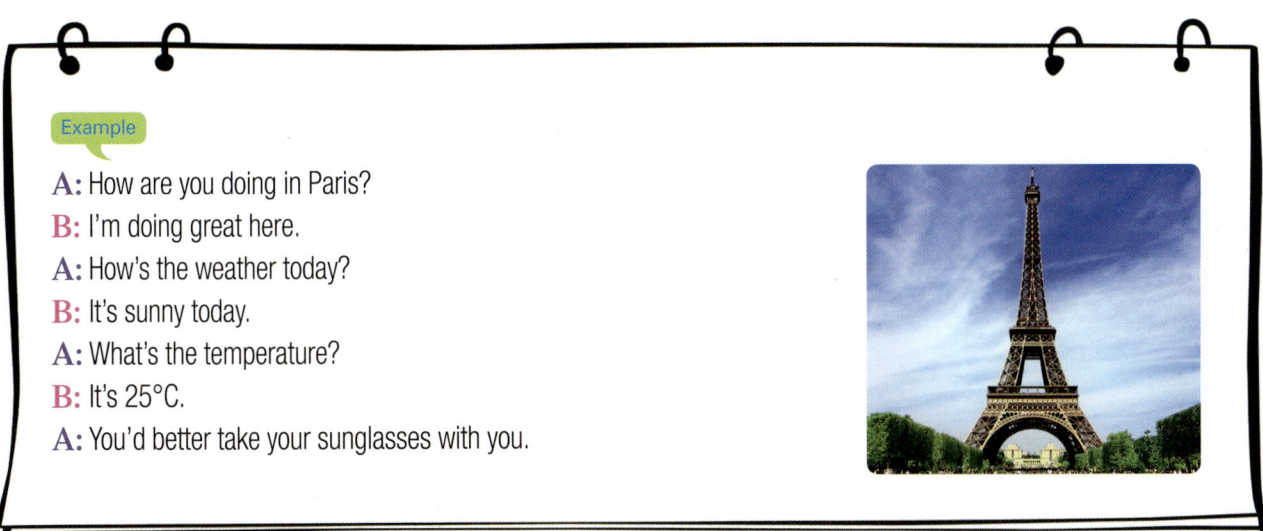

Example

A: How are you doing in Paris?
B: I'm doing great here.
A: How's the weather today?
B: It's sunny today.
A: What's the temperature?
B: It's 25°C.
A: You'd better take your sunglasses with you.

C Talk with your partner about the weather where you are today.

Lesson 4 · 31

Lesson 5: Which season do you like the best?

Warm-Up What month is it? What is the season?
Which sports do you like? Do you prefer summer or winter sports?

Dialogue Listen to the dialogue and practice.

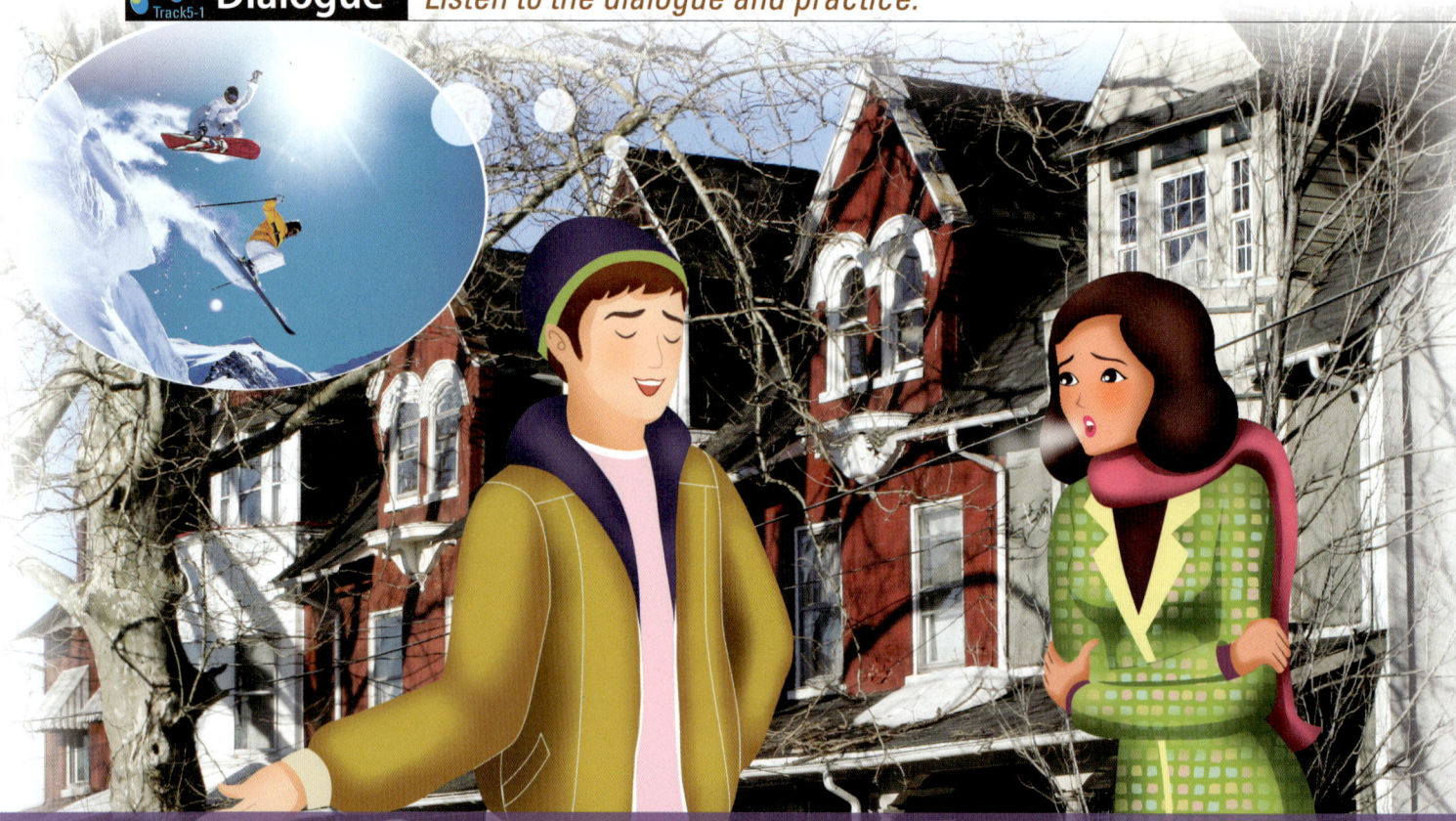

Michael: Linda, are you OK? You're shivering.
Linda: Yes, but it's so cold outside. Don't you think so?
Michael: Yes, I think winter is coming. I'm so excited!
Linda: Why are you excited?
Michael: Because winter is my favorite season.
Linda: Really? What do you like to do in winter?
Michael: I like to go skiing and snowboarding in winter. What about you? Which season do you like the best?
Linda: I like summer best.
Michael: Why? Do you like hot and humid weather?
Linda: No, I don't like hot and humid weather. But, I like almost every summer sport.
Michael: What summer sports do you like?
Linda: Hmm … I like swimming, scuba diving, and water skiing.

Language Focus

Seasons	
What's your favorite season?	My favorite season is spring. Spring is my favorite season.
Which season do you like (the) best?	I like autumn (the) best.

Seasonal Activities	
What do you like to do in summer?	I like to go rafting in summer.
What activities do you enjoy doing in winter?	I enjoy skiing in winter.

Pronunciation
Listen to the words and practice saying them.

ea
- /e/
  - weather, head, deaf, healthy
  - bread, sweat, leather, feather
- /i:/
  - season, eat, read, meat
  - peach, dream, steam, leaf

Talk 1

A Match the weather conditions with the seasons. Some weather conditions can be used more than once.

| sunny | cloudy | clear | windy | rainy | snowy | hot |
| warm | cool | cold | freezing | dry | humid | muggy |

B Roleplay conversations with a partner, referring to the pictures below.

Example
A: Which season do you like the best?
B: I like autumn the best.
A: Why do you like autumn?
B: Because I like cool weather.

Talk 2

A Check (✓) the seasons that match with the activities. Some activities can be checked more than once.

	Spring	Summer	Autumn/Fall	Winter
snowboarding	☐	☐	☐	☐
mountain climbing	☐	☐	☐	☐
taking photos	☐	☐	☐	☐
planting flowers	☐	☐	☐	☐
skiing	☐	☐	☐	☐
going on a picnic	☐	☐	☐	☐
windsurfing	☐	☐	☐	☐
skating	☐	☐	☐	☐
rafting	☐	☐	☐	☐
bungee jumping	☐	☐	☐	☐
going camping	☐	☐	☐	☐
swimming in the ocean	☐	☐	☐	☐
going for a drive	☐	☐	☐	☐
water skiing	☐	☐	☐	☐

B Roleplay conversations with a partner, referring to the pictures below.

Example

A: What's your favorite season?
A: Why is spring your favorite season?
A: What activities do you enjoy doing in spring?

B: Spring is my favorite season.
B: Because I like warm weather.
B: I enjoy planting flowers in spring.

i Speak

A Complete the table, using your own personal information.

B Ask three classmates questions to complete the table below.

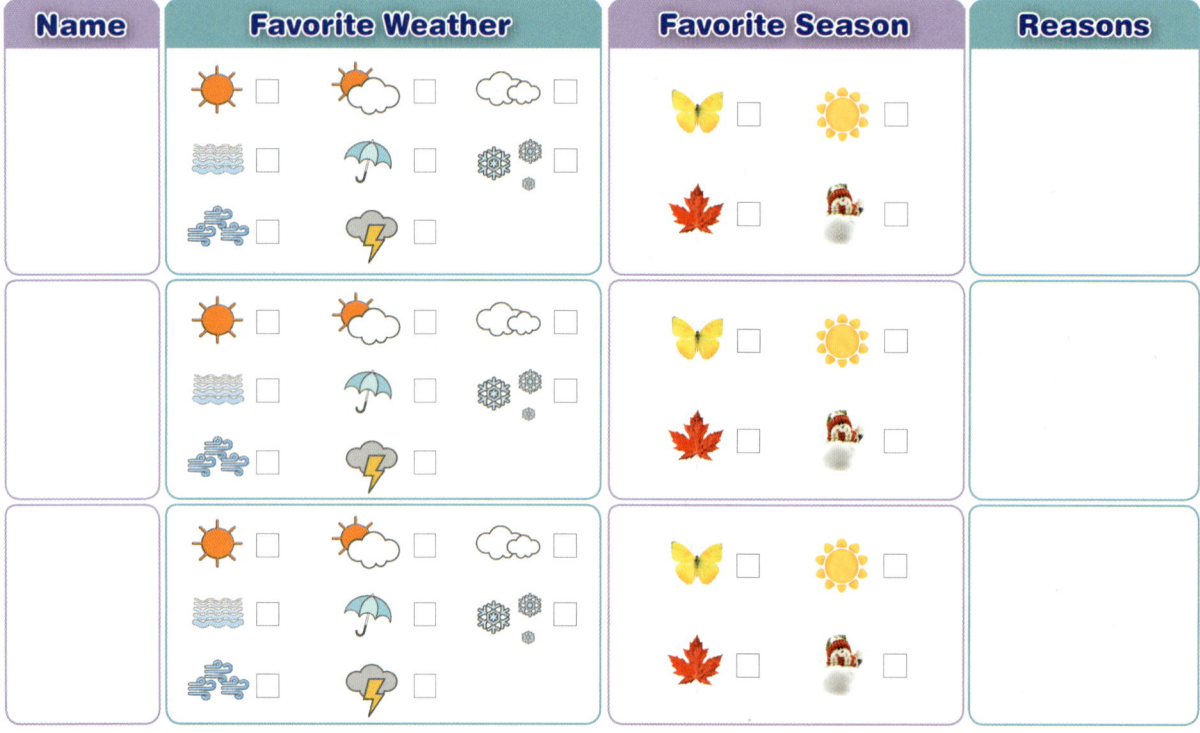

Example

A: What's your favorite weather?
B: I like sunny weather.
A: And what's your favorite season?
B: Summer is my favorite season.
A: Oh, really? Why is that?
B: Because I like going to the beach and swimming in the ocean.

 **Speak & Listen**

A 🎧 Listen to four people talking about their favorite seasons. Complete the table below.

	Vivian	**Edward**	**Jenny**	**Noel**
City	Auckland	Vancouver	Glasgow	Tokyo
Favorite Season				
Weather conditions				

B 🎧 Listen again and check (✓) the activities that the people like doing in their favorite seasons.

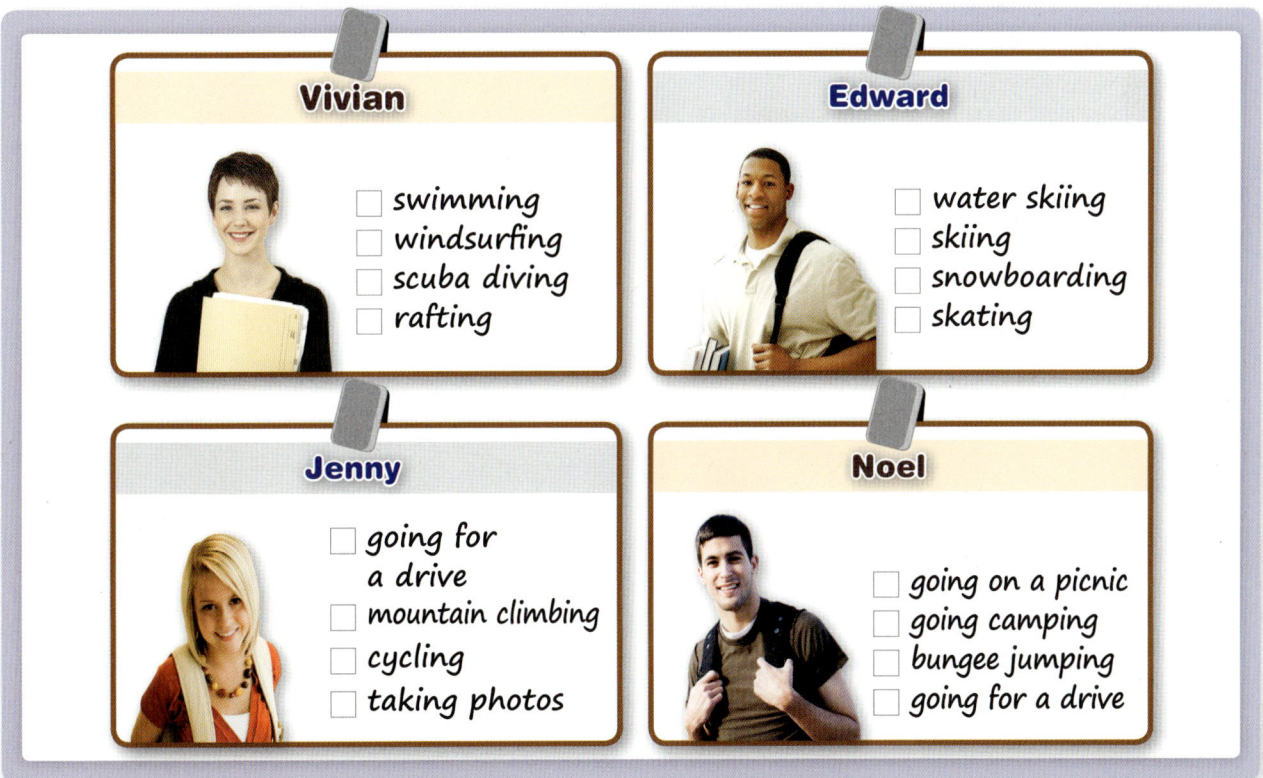

Vivian
☐ swimming
☐ windsurfing
☐ scuba diving
☐ rafting

Edward
☐ water skiing
☐ skiing
☐ snowboarding
☐ skating

Jenny
☐ going for a drive
☐ mountain climbing
☐ cycling
☐ taking photos

Noel
☐ going on a picnic
☐ going camping
☐ bungee jumping
☐ going for a drive

C Talk with your partner about your favorite season and activities. Include the information below.

☐ name
☐ favorite season
☐ favorite and least favorite activities in that season
☐ place you live
☐ weather conditions

Lesson 5 · 37

Lesson 6: How many people are there in your family?

Warm-Up
Do you have a small family or a large family?
Do you think it is better to have a large family or a small family?

Dialogue Listen to the dialogue and practice.

Peter: What are you doing this weekend?
Erin: I'm going on a family trip.
Peter: That sounds fun! Where are you going?
Erin: We're all going to the east coast. There's going to be a lot of people.
Peter: Really? How many people are there in your family?
Erin: There are seven people in my family, including my brother-in-law and nephew.
Peter: Wow! What a big family! Are you the eldest?
Erin: No. I'm the middle child. I have an elder sister and a younger brother. My sister got married three years ago and I have a nephew.
Peter: Do you and your siblings all get along well?
Erin: Yes, we do, because we have a lot in common. I can't wait to go on the family trip.
Peter: It sounds great. Enjoy the trip!

Language Focus

Family Members

How many people are there in your family? How many brothers and sisters do you have?	There are four people in my family. I have one sister and two brothers.
Do you have any siblings?	Yes, I have two sisters. No, I'm an only child.
What relation is she to you? How is she related to you?	She's my aunt.

Birth Order

Are you the eldest in your family?	Yes, I'm the eldest. No, I'm the second oldest. No, I'm the middle child. No, I'm the youngest.

 **Pronunciation** *Listen to the words and practice saying them.*

☐ **f**
| family | farm | father | find |
| foam | fork | funny | ferry |

☐ **p**
| people | palm | paper | pencil |
| picture | pork | paint | pepper |

☐ **tr**
| trip | tree | truth | train |
| trash | truck | trend | triangle |

Lesson 6 · 39

Talk 1

A How is each person related to Peter? Complete the blue spaces in the family tree, using the words in the box.

| mother-in-law | daughter | nephew | brother-in-law | sister-in-law |
| niece | wife | father-in-law | son | |

B How is each person related to Kelly? Complete in the green spaces in the family tree in **A**, using the words in the box.

| uncle | father | grandfather | cousin | mother |
| younger brother | elder brother | aunt | grandmother | cousin |

C Practice the dialogue with a partner, referring to the family tree in **A**.

> Example
> A: How is Jenny related to Ben?
> B: She's Ben's aunt.

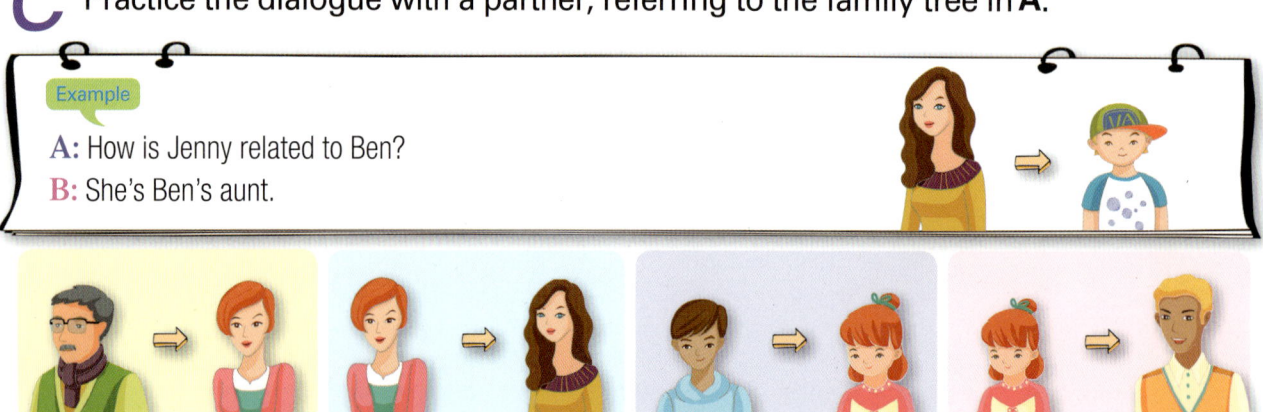

Talk 2

A Write the name of each person next to the words that describe their birth order.

Birth Order

- the second youngest
- the youngest
- the second oldest
- the middle child
- the eldest

B Talk with your partner about their birth order, referring to the information in **A**.

Example

A: Does Nicole have any brothers or sisters?
B: Yes, she does.
A: How many siblings does she have?
B: She has two younger sisters and two younger brothers.
A: I see. So, she's the eldest, right?
B: That's right. She's the eldest.

i Speak

A Complete the form, using your own personal information.

Name: _____		Date of Birth: _____	
Family Members			
Relationship	Name	Age	Occupation

B Ask your partner questions to complete the form.

Name: _____		Date of Birth: _____	
Family Members			
Relationship	Name	Age	Occupation

A: So, tell me about your family. How many people are there in your family?

B: There are five people in my family: my parents, my older sister, my younger sister, and me.

A: I see. I want to know more about each of your family members.

B: Sure. My father's name is Jun-ho Lee. He is 52 years old. He is a doctor.

 Speak & Listen

A Listen and fill in Jason's family tree, using the names below.

| John | Helen | Julie | Adam | Suzie | Sam | Chris |

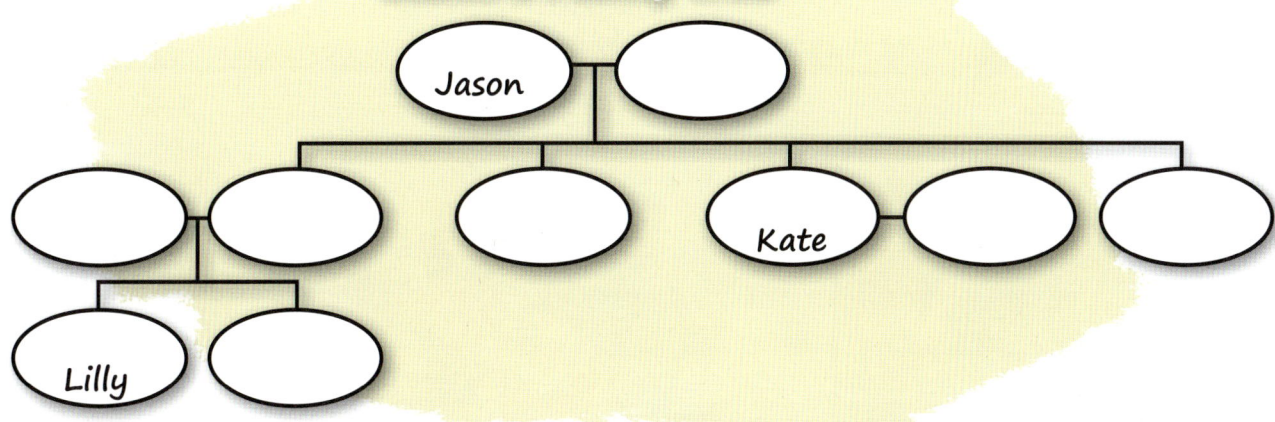

B Listen again and write what each person does.

Name	Occupation
Jason	accountant
Helen	
Adam	
John	
Suzie	

Name	Occupation
Sam	
Lilly	
Kate	
Chris	
Julie	

C Talk with your partner about Jason's family, using the information in **A** and **B**.

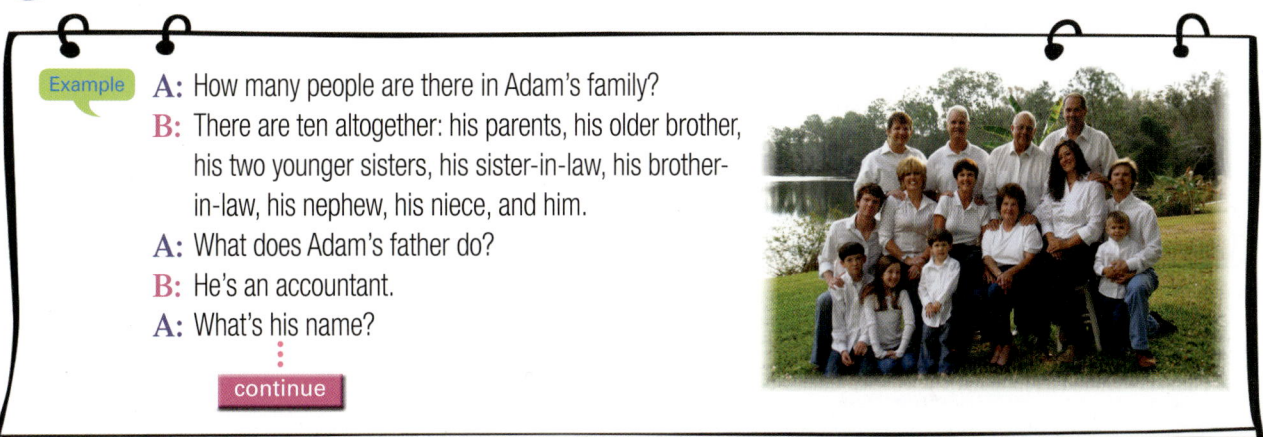

Example
A: How many people are there in Adam's family?
B: There are ten altogether: his parents, his older brother, his two younger sisters, his sister-in-law, his brother-in-law, his nephew, his niece, and him.
A: What does Adam's father do?
B: He's an accountant.
A: What's his name?

continue

Lesson 6 • 43

Lesson 7
Who do you take after?

Warm-Up   Do you think you look more like your father or your mother? How many siblings do you have? Who do they take after?

Dialogue   Listen to the dialogue and practice.

Sam: Is this a picture of your family?
Judy: Yes, it is. I took the picture last year.
Sam: I see. You really look like your mom, don't you?
Judy: Yes. I have my mom's eyes and nose.
Sam: And, I think you and your younger sister look alike too.
Judy: Yes, we do. We all take after my mother and we have a lot in common as well.
Sam: I'm sure you do. Who does your older brother resemble more, your father or your mother? I can't really tell from the picture.
Judy: He resembles my father more.
Sam: Oh, that's right.
Judy: Who do you take after, Sam?
Sam: I take after my father. I'll show you a family picture tomorrow.

Language Focus

Resemblance I

Who do you take after?
Who does he look like?
Who do you resemble more, your father or your mother?

I **take after** my father.
He **looks like** his mom.
I **resemble** my father **more**.

Resemblance II

I have my mom's eyes.
My sister and I look alike.
He gets his writing skills from his mother.
They both have a talent for music.
My younger brother and I have a lot / nothing in common.

 Pronunciation *Listen to the words and practice saying them.*

☐ **tu** (/tʃə/)
picture   actually   punctual   acupuncture

☐ **su** (/ʃʊ/)
sure   sugar   ensure   insurance

☐ **Linking Sounds**
as well   after all   at all   as long as   as soon as

Talk 1

A Decide if you agree or disagree with each statements. Refer to the pictures.

Grandmother   **Father**   **Mother**   **Peter**   **Emily**

	Agree	Disagree
❶ Emily's father looks like her grandmother.	☐	☐
❷ Emily and her mother look alike.	☐	☐
❸ Emily has her father's nose.	☐	☐
❹ Peter has his mother's eyes.	☐	☐
❺ Emily gets her lips from her mother.	☐	☐
❻ Peter and Emily have the same nose.	☐	☐

B Practice the dialogue with a partner, using the family trees below.

> **Example**
> **A:** Who does Brian take after?
> **B:** I think he takes after his father. He has his father's eyes.
> **A:** Yes, I agree.

Cathy's Family   **Ian's Family**   **Anna's Family**

Talk 2

A Match the names in **bold** with the people in the pictures.

- Mike and **Ken** are brothers. They both take after their father. They have his big nose.
- Susie and **Emma** are twins. They don't have much in common, but they both have the same big brown eyes.
- Tom and **John** are cousins. They get their athletic ability from their grandfather.
- Judy and **Liz** are sisters. They don't look alike, but they both have a talent for music.

Mike   **Susie**   **Tom**   **Judy**

B Talk with your partner about how people resemble each other, using the information in **A**.

Example
A: Are Tony and Laura related?
B: Yes. They're siblings.
A: Really? Do they have anything in common?
B: They both have a talent for numbers.

i Speak

A Talk with your partner about any resemblance between Eric's family, referring to the picture. Follow the example dialogue.

- ❶ Eric – Eric's mother
- ❷ Eric's nephew – Eric's sister
- ❸ Eric's nephew – Eric's brother-in-law
- ❹ Eric's niece – Eric's sister

Example

❶ Eric – Eric's mother

A: Is there any resemblance between Eric and his mother?
B: He has his mother's eyes and nose. / He gets his eyes and nose from his mother.

B Talk with your partner about your family members and the resemblances you share with them.

Example

A: How many people are there in your family?
B: There are four people in my family: my father, my mother, my younger sister, and me.
A: Who do you take after?
B: I take after my father. I have my father's eyes and nose.
A: Is there any resemblance between you and your mother?
B: Well, I think I get my writing skills from my mother.

 **Speak & Listen**

A 🎧 Listen to the information about James Parker. Match the names with the people, and write each person's relationship to James Parker.

| Alison | Erin | Lauren |

James Parker

| Name: | Name: | Name: |
| Relationship: | Relationship: | Relationship: |

B 🎧 Listen again and complete the table. Then ask your partner questions to check your answers.

	True	False	Correction (if false)
• Lauren has her father's nose.	☐	☐	
• Lauren and Alison look alike.	☐	☐	
• Alison does not resemble her father.	☐	☐	
• Alison gets her writing ability from her mother.	☐	☐	
• Erin is younger than Alison.	☐	☐	
• Erin gets her powerful voice from her mother.	☐	☐	

Example
A: Does Lauren have her father's nose?
B: No, she doesn't. She has her father's dark brown eyes.

continue

Lesson 8
What's he like?

Warm-Up Who is your best friend? What is he/she like?
What kind of personality do you think you have?

Dialogue Listen to the dialogue and practice.

Tony: Pamela, are you seeing anyone at the moment?
Pamela: No, I'm still single. Why?
Tony: Do you want me to set up a blind date for you with a friend of mine?
Pamela: Well, what's he like?
Tony: He's outgoing. He likes to hang out with people. Also, he's a thoughtful person. He cares a lot about other people.
Pamela: He sounds like a nice person.
Tony: Yes, he is. So, do you want to have a blind date with him?
Pamela: Hmm … does he have a sense of humor? I like people with a good sense of humor.
Tony: Fortunately, yes, he does. He was the clown of the class when we were in junior high.
Pamela: OK then. Why not? He sounds like a nice guy.
Tony: I hope you two get along well.
Pamela: I hope so, too.

Language Focus

Personality Types

outgoing	friendly	shy	arrogant
active	adventurous	selfish	boring
generous	humorous	lazy	greedy
kind	diligent	rude	naughty
modest	thoughtful	moody	mean

Questions About Personality

What is he like?	He's **outgoing** / **generous** / **humorous** / **adventurous** / **rude**.
What is her personality like?	She's **an active person** / **a kind person** / **a greedy person**.
How would you describe your personality?	I would say I'm **a friendly and funny person**.

Pronunciation

Listen to the words and practice saying them.

☐ **ly**
late**ly**	friend**ly**	fortunate**ly**	recent**ly**
love**ly**	tru**ly**	definite**ly**	certain**ly**

☐ **bl**
blind	**bl**ack	**bl**ond	**bl**ock
blue	**bl**ank	**bl**end	**bl**ossom

☐ **hu** (/hjuː/)
humor	**hu**morous	**hu**man	**hu**mane
huge	**hu**mid	**hu**midity	**hu**mility

Talk 1

A Match the words that have opposite meanings.

| boring | diligent | modest | generous | arrogant | shy |
| mean | kind | humorous | lazy | greedy | outgoing |

  Ian
 Cathy

  Emma
Tom

  John
Fiona

B Talk with your partner about each person in **A**, using the pictures above.

Example

A: Is he Ian?
A: He seems generous.
A: Why? What's he really like?
A: Wow! I didn't know that.

B: Yes, he is.
B: You got him wrong.
B: Really he's greedy.
B: Yes, so the first impression isn't always right.

Talk 2

A Match the words with the descriptions.

thoughtful	rude	naughty	lazy	moody
adventurous	generous	active	greedy	diligent
humorous	outgoing	selfish		

- **Dustin** likes to try new things and likes challenges.
- **Laura** likes to hang out with people.
- **Rick** cares about other people.
- **Emily** thinks only about herself and doesn't care about other people.
- **Tony** speaks and acts harshly to people.
- **Brian** enjoys all sorts of activities and sports.
- **Nancy** starts the day early and works hard.
- **Vivian** behaves badly and never does what she is told.
- **James** gets up late and doesn't like to do anything difficult.
- **Hannah** suddenly becomes happy, sad or angry.
- **Luke** has a sense of humor.
- **Cathy** likes to help other people and share things with them.
- **Kevin** always wants more.

adventurous

B Talk with your partner about each person's personality in **A**.

Example
A: Do you know Dustin?
B: Yes, I know him. Why?
A: What's his personality like?
B: Hmm ... I would say he's an adventurous person.
A: Could you be more specific?
B: He likes to try new things and likes challenges.

i Speak

A Complete the table, using your own personal information.

Name	Personality Type	Reason

B Ask four classmates questions to complete the table.

Name	Personality Type	Reason

Example
A: Excuse me, Jenna. How would you describe your personality?
B: I would say I'm a shy person.
A: Why do you describe yourself as a shy person?
B: Well, because I don't like to be around lots of people at the same time. What about you? How would you describe your personality?
A: I would say …

continue

 Speak & Listen

A 🎧 Listen to the dialogue. Match the names with the people.

| Jean | Sue | Rick | Aaron |

B 🎧 Listen to the dialogue again. Complete the table.

First Impression				
Real Personality				

C Practice the dialogue with a partner, using the information in **B**. Then talk about the personalities of your classmates in the same way.

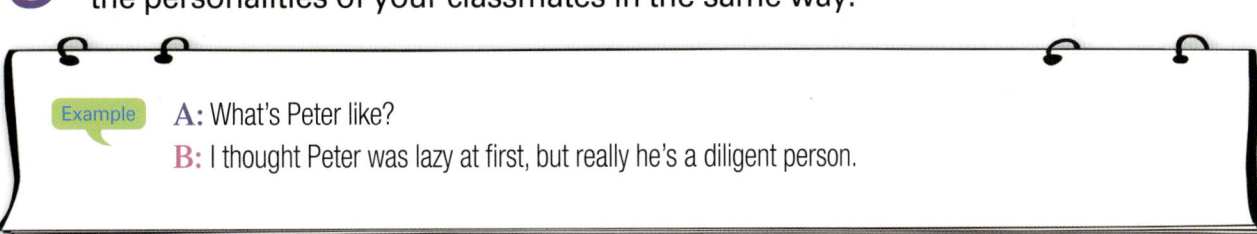

Example
A: What's Peter like?
B: I thought Peter was lazy at first, but really he's a diligent person.

Lesson 9: Do you ever use dental floss?

Warm-Up
Are you a vegetarian or a meat eater?
Do you think you are a healthy person? What, if anything, do you do to stay healthy?

 Dialogue Listen to the dialogue and practice.

Annie: Good morning, Roy!
Roy: Ahhh … good morning.
Annie: Are you OK? What's wrong?
Roy: My teeth are sore. I have toothache.
Annie: Oh, no. I've had that pain before. Can you chew?
Roy: No. I can't chew anything.
Annie: How often do you brush your teeth?
Roy: Three times a day.
Annie: Do you ever use dental floss after you brush your teeth?
Roy: No, I never use it.
Annie: You should use dental floss. It keeps your teeth really healthy.
Roy: Where do you buy that?
Annie: You can buy it in any convenience store. But first you'd better go see a dentist.
Roy: I will. Thanks.

Language Focus

Yes/No Questions with Frequency Adverbs

Do you **sometimes / often / usually / regularly** go jogging?	Yes, I **sometimes/often/usually/regularly** go jogging. No, I **rarely/never** go jogging.
Does he **sometimes / often / usually / regularly** go hiking?	Yes, he **sometimes/often/usually/regularly** goes hiking. No, he **rarely/never** goes hiking.
Do you **ever** exercise?	Yes, I do. I **sometimes/regularly** exercise. No, I don't. I **rarely/never** exercise.

Wh- Questions with Frequency Adverbs

Where do you **usually** go swimming?	I **usually** go swimming **in the sports center**.
What does he **usually** have for breakfast?	He **usually** has **Korean food** for breakfast.
Who does she **usually** have lunch with?	She **usually** has lunch **with Jenny**.
When do you **usually** work out?	I **usually** work out **on the weekends**.
How do they **usually** get to work?	They **usually** get to work **by bus**.
How often do you get a medical checkup?	I get a medical checkup **once a year**.

Pronunciation
Listen to the words and practice saying them.

☐ **Silent w**
wrong   write   wrap   wrestle   wreck

☐ **br**
brush   brother   brown   breeze   bread

☐ **fl**
floss   flute   flower   flash   flood

Lesson 9 · 57

Talk 1

A Match the words with the pictures. Then check (✓) the foods that you think are unhealthy.

soda	seafood	fast food	fruits
vegetables	instant noodles	dairy products	sweets
garlic	snacks	pizza	nuts

B Roleplay conversations with your partner, using the information below.

Example

A: Do you like soda?

If Yes

B: Yes, I do. I sometimes/regularly drink soda.
A: Exactly how often do you drink soda?
B: Probably three times a week.
A: That isn't very good for your health.

If No

B: No, I don't. I never/rarely drink soda.
A: That's good!

 sometimes / once a week

 rarely

 regularly / twice a week

 never

 sometimes / three times a month

Talk 2

A Match the questions with the answers.

Questions
1. **Who** do you usually eat breakfast **with**?
2. **Do** you usually eat breakfast?
3. **What** do you usually eat for breakfast?
4. **Where** do you usually eat breakfast?

Answers
- **Yes**, I usually eat breakfast. ☐
- I usually eat **an omelet** for breakfast. ☐
- I usually eat breakfast **at home**. ☐
- I usually eat breakfast **alone**. ☐

B Roleplay conversations with your partner, using the information below.

Example

A: Do you usually go jogging in the morning?
A: When do you usually go jogging then?
A: Oh, I see.

B: No, I never go jogging in the morning.
B: I usually go jogging in the evening.

go to bed late?

drink a glass of water in the morning?

go hiking alone?

go jogging in the park?

work out alone?

eat fast food for dinner?

i Speak

A Complete the questionnaire, circling your answers. Then add up your score to find out how healthy you are.

✓ Health Check!

① **Do you ever smoke?**
never 3   sometimes 2   often 1   regularly 0

② **Do you ever drink alcohol?**
never 3   sometimes 2   often 1   regularly 0

③ **Do you ever eat vegetables?**
never 0   sometimes 1   often 2   regularly 3

④ **Do you ever eat fruits?**
never 0   sometimes 1   often 2   regularly 3

⑤ **Do you ever drink eight glasses of water in a day?**
never 0   sometimes 1   often 2   regularly 3

⑥ **Do you ever skip a meal?**
never 0   sometimes 1   often 2   regularly 3

⑦ **Do you ever use dental floss?**
never 0   sometimes 1   often 2   regularly 3

⑧ **Do you ever exercise?**
never 0   sometimes 1   often 2   regularly 3

⑨ **Do you ever meditate?**
never 0   sometimes 1   often 2   regularly 3

⑩ **Do you ever get 8 hours' sleep?**
never 0   sometimes 1   often 2   regularly 3

⑪ **Do you ever get a medical checkup?**
never 0   sometimes 1   often 2   regularly 3

Your score

- **22–33 points**   You are a very healthy person. You should be proud of yourself. Keep up the good work!
- **11–21 points**   You could be healthier if you tried a little bit harder. Try to exercise more and eat a balanced diet!
- **0–10 points**   You'd better start thinking more about your health. Love yourself more and take better care of yourself!

B Ask your partner questions, referring to the questionnaire in **A**.

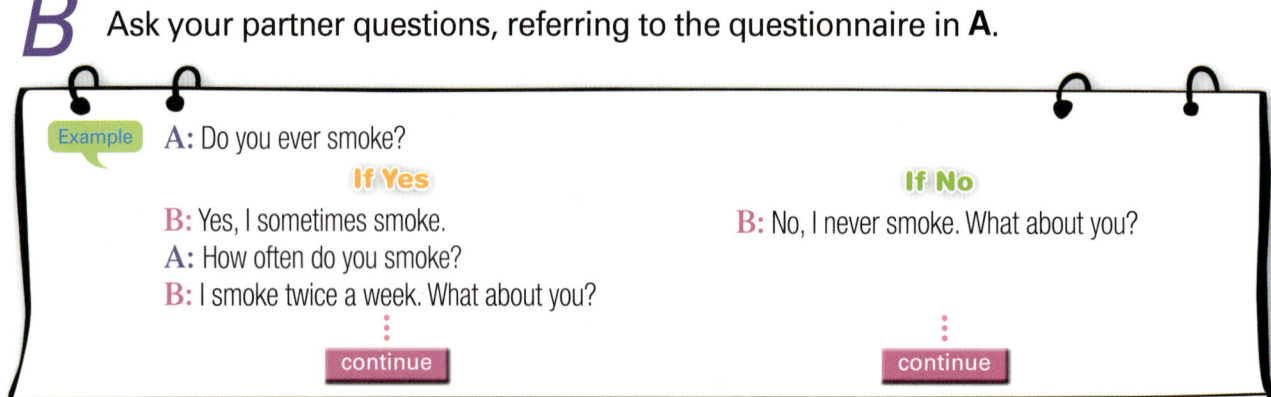

Example
A: Do you ever smoke?

If Yes
B: Yes, I sometimes smoke.
A: How often do you smoke?
B: I smoke twice a week. What about you?
⋮
continue

If No
B: No, I never smoke. What about you?
⋮
continue

Speak & Listen

A 🎧 Listen to the dialogue. Check (✓) the things that Victoria does to stay healthy.

B 🎧 Listen again and complete the table. Then ask your partner questions to check your answers.

Does she ever … ?	Yes/No	How often does she … ?
skip a meal	Yes ☐ No ☐	
drink ten glasses of water	Yes ☐ No ☐	
do yoga	Yes ☐ No ☐	
work out at the gym	Yes ☐ No ☐	
dance	Yes ☐ No ☐	
go hiking	Yes ☐ No ☐	

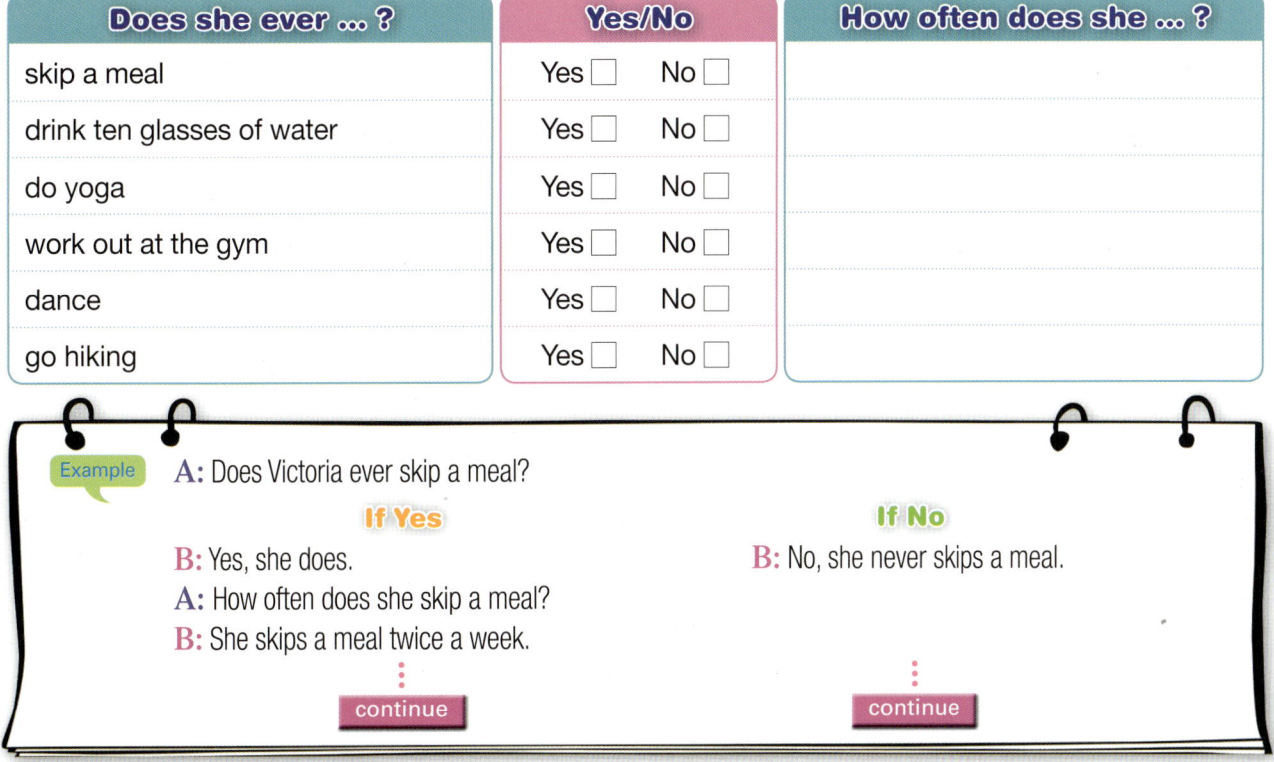

Example
A: Does Victoria ever skip a meal?

If Yes
B: Yes, she does.
A: How often does she skip a meal?
B: She skips a meal twice a week.
⋮
continue

If No
B: No, she never skips a meal.
⋮
continue

C Tell the class what you do to stay healthy, and say how often you do it.

Lesson 10
What does it look like?

Warm-Up Describe an item that you own to your partner.
Try to guess what item your partner is describing.

Dialogue Listen to the dialogue and practice.

Molly: Hey William, did you see my MP3 player anywhere?
William: Your MP3 player? The red one?
Molly: No, I bought a new one yesterday. The red one is pretty old.
William: What does your new MP3 player look like?
Molly: It's rectangular and pink.
William: Hmm ... I saw something pink on the dining table last night.
Molly: Really? I'll check right away. [pause]
William: Did you find it? Is it there?
Molly: No, that's not my MP3 player. That's my cell phone.
William: Don't worry. I'm sure it'll turn up somewhere.

Language Focus

Describing Things	
What does it look like?	It's small, square, and flat.
What shape is it?	It's round / square / rectangular / triangular / oval / flat / box-shaped.
What color is it?	It's silver / light green / gold / purple / gray / yellow.
What is it made of?	It's made of wood / plastic / cotton / wool / steel / silver / gold / leather / glass / paper / rubber / metal / clay.
What do you use it for?	**You use it for** mak**ing** food. / **You use it to** make food.
What is it used for?	**It's used for** mak**ing** food. / **It's used to** make food.

Pronunciation

Listen to the words and practice saying them.

☐ **Silent gh**
bought	caught	daughter	neighbor
though	straight	weight	through

☐ **ou/au (/ɔː/)**
bought	fought	thought	sought
cause	caught	taught	sauce

☐ **tt (/t/)**
pretty	better	matter	butter
bitter	letter	cutter	bottle

Talk 1

A What does each item look like? Match the words with the pictures.

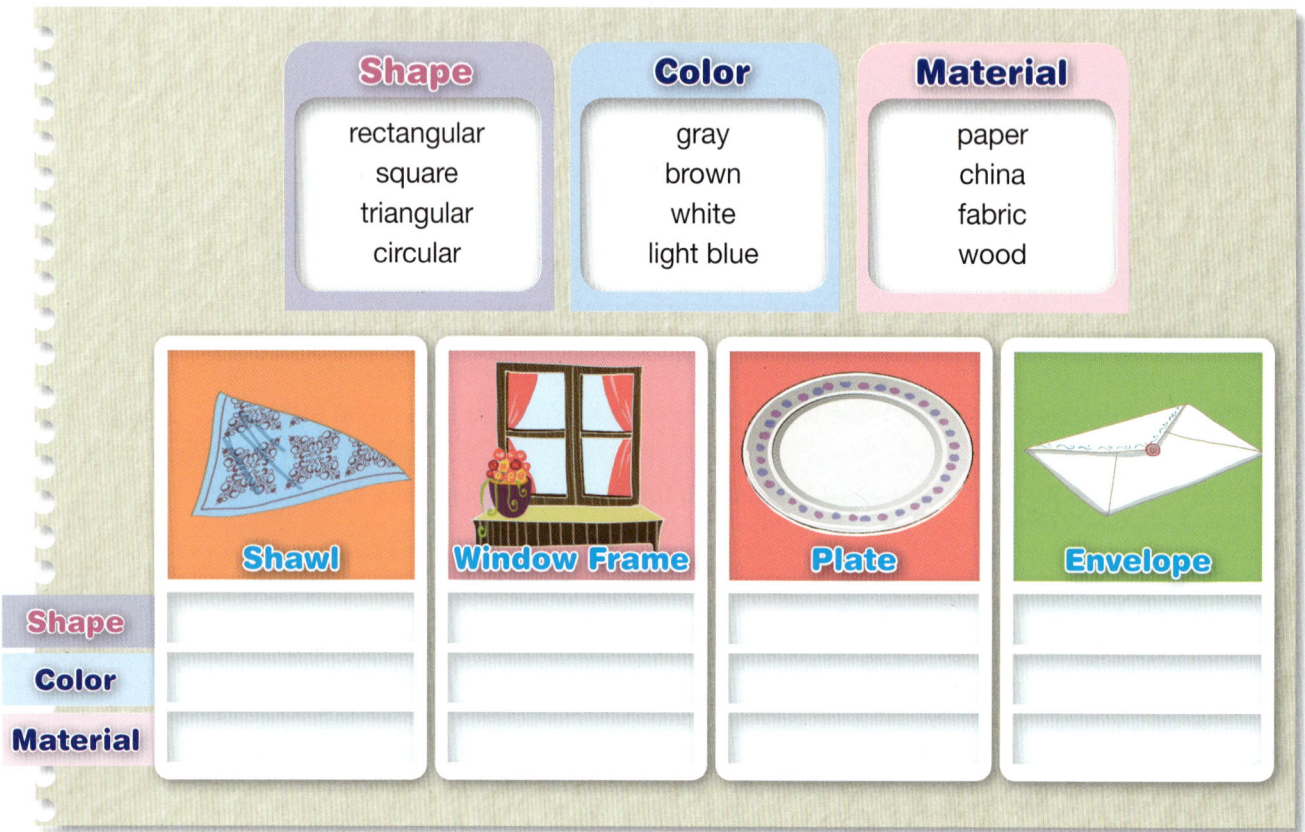

B Describe the items in **A** to your partner.

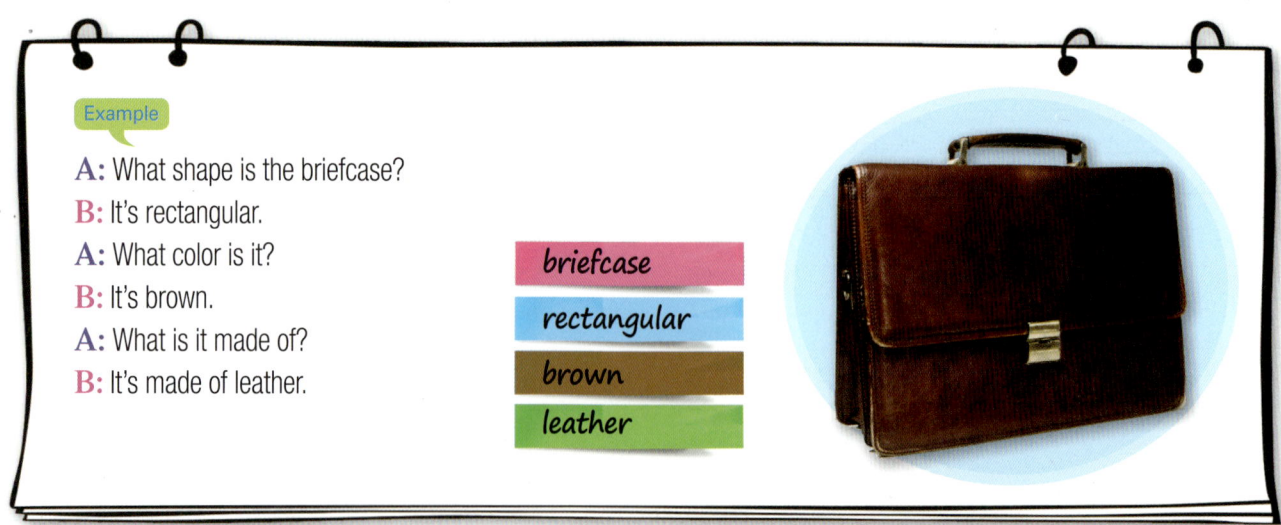

Example

A: What shape is the briefcase?
B: It's rectangular.
A: What color is it?
B: It's brown.
A: What is it made of?
B: It's made of leather.

briefcase
rectangular
brown
leather

Talk 2

A What are the items below called? What are they used for? Match the words with the pictures.

Names of Items	vacuum cleaner	wallet	microwave oven	basketball
Uses	hold money	play basketball	clean the house	heat up food

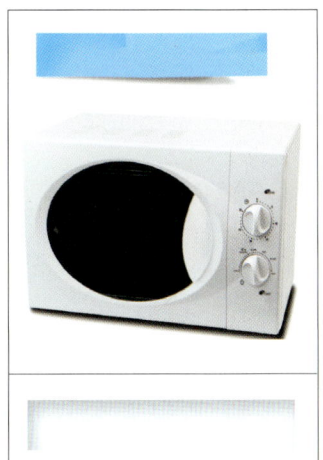

B Describe the items in **A** to your partner.

Example

A: What is this item called?
B: It's called a washing machine.
A: What is it used for?
B: It's used to wash clothes. /
   It's used for washing clothes.

washing machine
wash clothes

i Speak

A Draw five items that you own. Do not let your partner see your drawings.

B Ask your partner questions to find out what he/she has drawn. You may only ask six questions, and answers must be either 'Yes' or 'No' only. Whoever finds out the most drawings is the winner. Follow the example below.

> **Example**
>
> **A:** Here is my first question. Is the item square? **B:** No, it isn't.
> **A:** Then, is it rectangular? **B:** No, it isn't.
> **A:** Is it circular? **B:** Yes, it is.
> **A:** Is it made of glass? **B:** No, it isn't.
> **A:** Is it made of steel? **B:** No, it isn't. You have only one question left!
> **A:** OK. Is it made of plastic? **B:** Yes, it is. It is made of plastic.
> **A:** Um … I think it's a button. **B:** Yes, it is. You win! / No, it isn't. You lose!

 **Speak & Listen**

A 🎧 Listen and match descriptions 1-6 with the pictures.

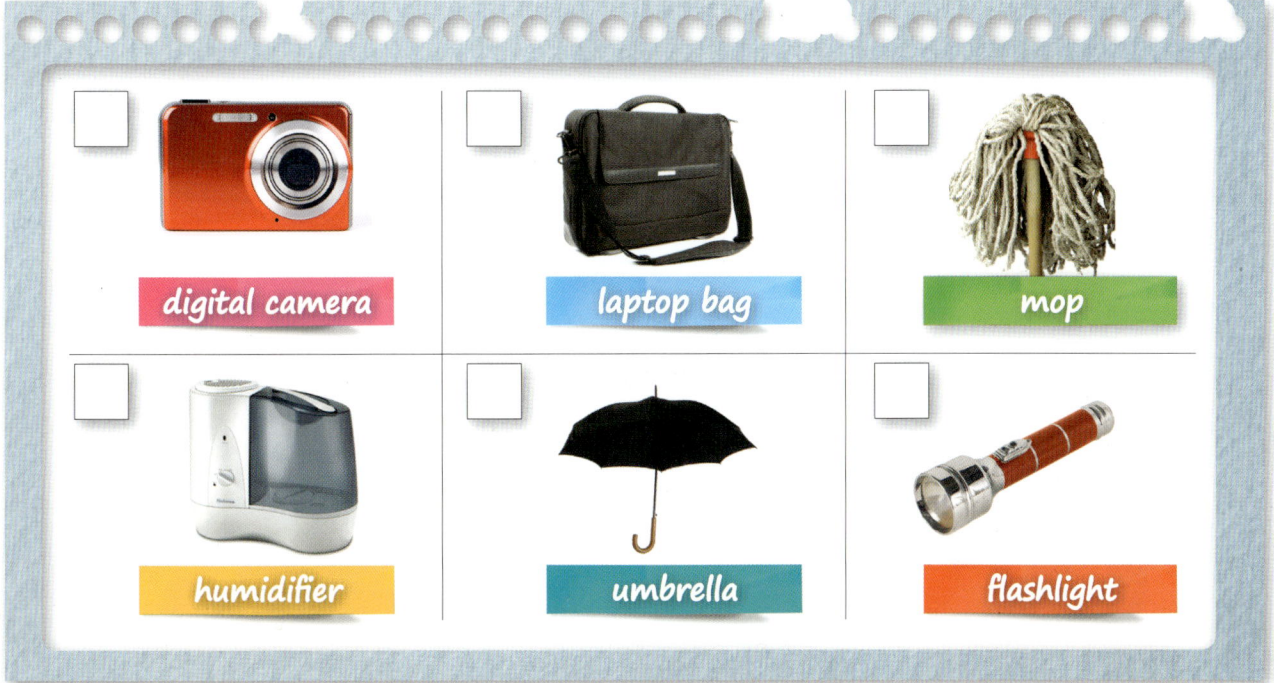

B 🎧 Listen again and write the uses of the items in **A**.

Name of Item	Use	Name of Item	Use
digital camera		humidifier	
laptop bag		umbrella	
mop		flashlight	

C Talk with your partner about the items and their uses in **A** and B.

Example
A: What does the alarm clock look like?
B: It's round and red. It has numbers on it.
A: What is it used for?
B: It's used for telling the time.

alarm clock

Lesson 11: It should be on the coffee table.

Warm-Up Describe a time when you lost something. Did you find it? How did losing something make you feel?

 **Dialogue** Listen to the dialogue and practice.

Paul: Rachel, where are you?
Rachel: I'm in the kitchen, sweetie. What's the matter?
Paul: Did you see today's newspaper? I can't find it anywhere.
Rachel: Did you check in the living room? It should be on the coffee table.
Paul: I've already checked there. There's nothing on the coffee table.
Rachel: That's weird. That's where I always put the paper.
Paul: Oh, I found it. It was under the table. It must have fallen on the floor.
Rachel: That's good to hear.
Paul: Oh, no!
Rachel: What's wrong?
Paul: It's all torn up. The cat must have been playing with it.

Language Focus

	Locations of Objects	
	Where are the toys?	**They are in** the box.
	Where is the watch?	**It is beside (next to)** the cell phone.
	Where is the pencil case?	**It is between** the book **and** the pen.
	Where is the mug? Where is the cat?	**It is on** the table. **It is under** the table.
	Where is the picture? Where is the couch?	**It is above** the couch. **It is below** the picture.
	Where are the shoes? Where are the socks?	**They are in front of** the socks. **They are behind** the shoes.

🎧 Pronunciation   Listen to the words and practice saying them.
Track11-2

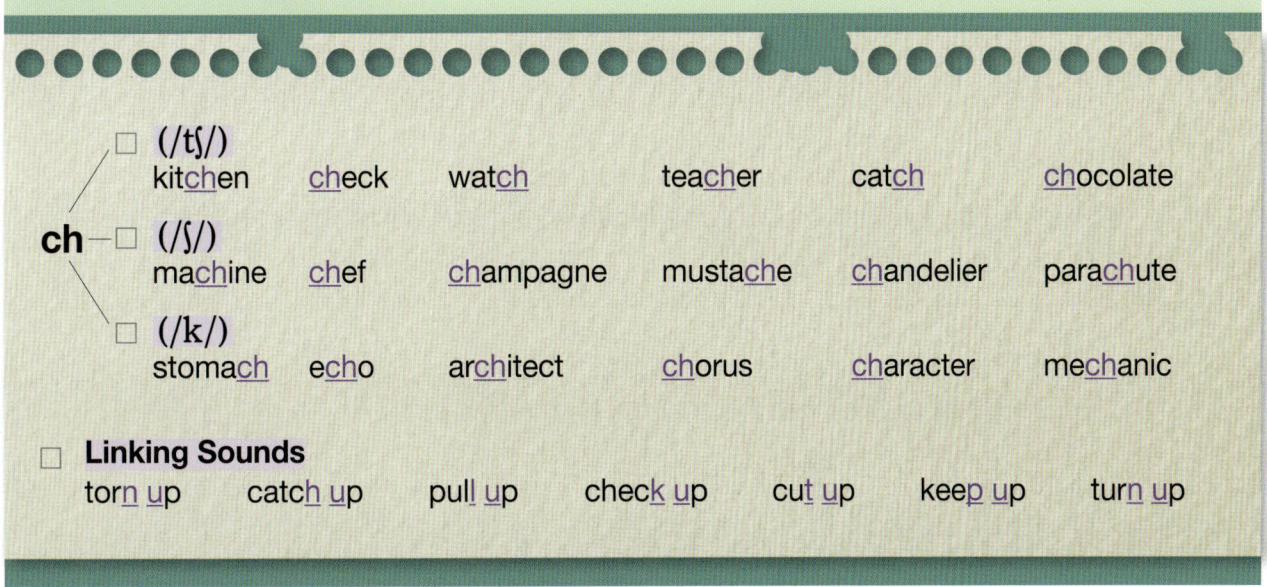

- ☐ (/tʃ/)
  ki**tch**en   **ch**eck   wa**tch**   tea**ch**er   ca**tch**   **ch**ocolate

ch ─ ☐ (/ʃ/)
  ma**ch**ine   **ch**ef   **ch**ampagne   musta**ch**e   **ch**andelier   para**ch**ute

- ☐ (/k/)
  stoma**ch**   e**ch**o   ar**ch**itect   **ch**orus   **ch**aracter   me**ch**anic

☐ **Linking Sounds**
tor**n** **u**p   catc**h** **u**p   pul**l** **u**p   chec**k** **u**p   cu**t** **u**p   kee**p** **u**p   tur**n** **u**p

Talk 1

A Match the words with the items in the picture.

- ⓐ clothes
- ⓑ mirror
- ⓒ chair
- ⓓ coins
- ⓔ teddy bear
- ⓕ magazine
- ⓖ pillow
- ⓗ lamp
- ⓘ closet
- ⓙ books
- ⓚ nightstand
- ⓛ cell phone
- ⓜ bed
- ⓝ poster
- ⓞ clock
- ⓟ computer
- ⓠ sneakers
- ⓡ trash can

B Ask your partner questions about the locations of the items in the picture. Follow the example below.

Example
A: Do you see the pen in the picture? Where is the pen?
B: It's on the floor. What about the keys? Where are the keys?
A: They're next to the pen.

continue

Talk 2

A Find the differences between Picture 1 and Picture 2.

B Talk with your partner about the differences between Picture 1 and Picture 2.

Example
A: Did you find any differences between the pictures?
B: Yes. There's a window in Picture 1, but there isn't a window in Picture 2. There's a painting instead.

continue

i Speak

A Draw a bedroom. Include the items in the box in your drawing. Do not let your partner see your drawing.

| closet | dresser | nightstand | clock | bookshelf |
| picture | lamp | television | stereo | computer |

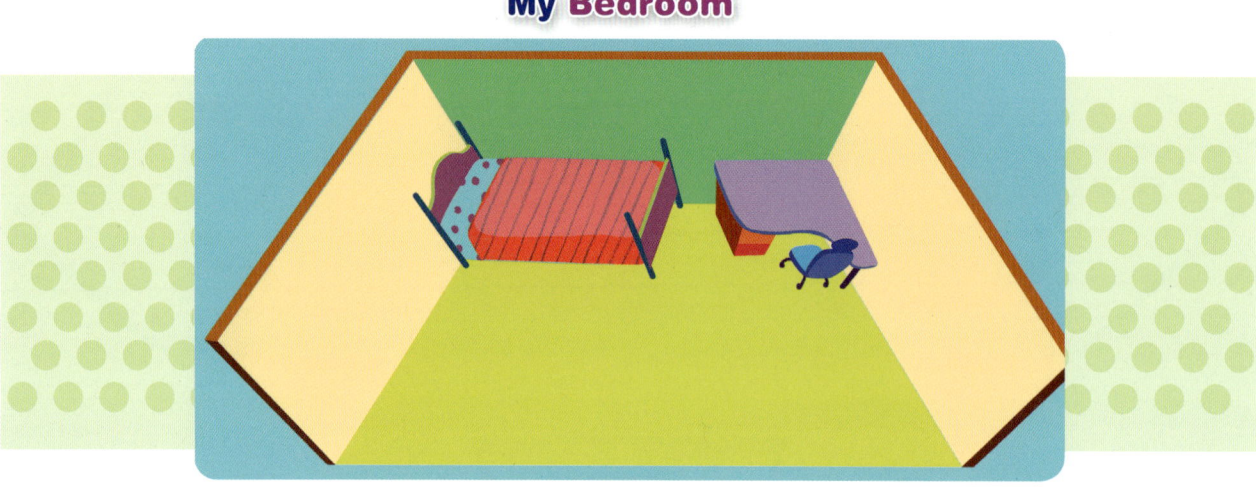

My Bedroom

B Ask your partner questions to draw his/her bedroom. Check your drawing by comparing it with your partner's drawing in **A**.

_____'s Bedroom

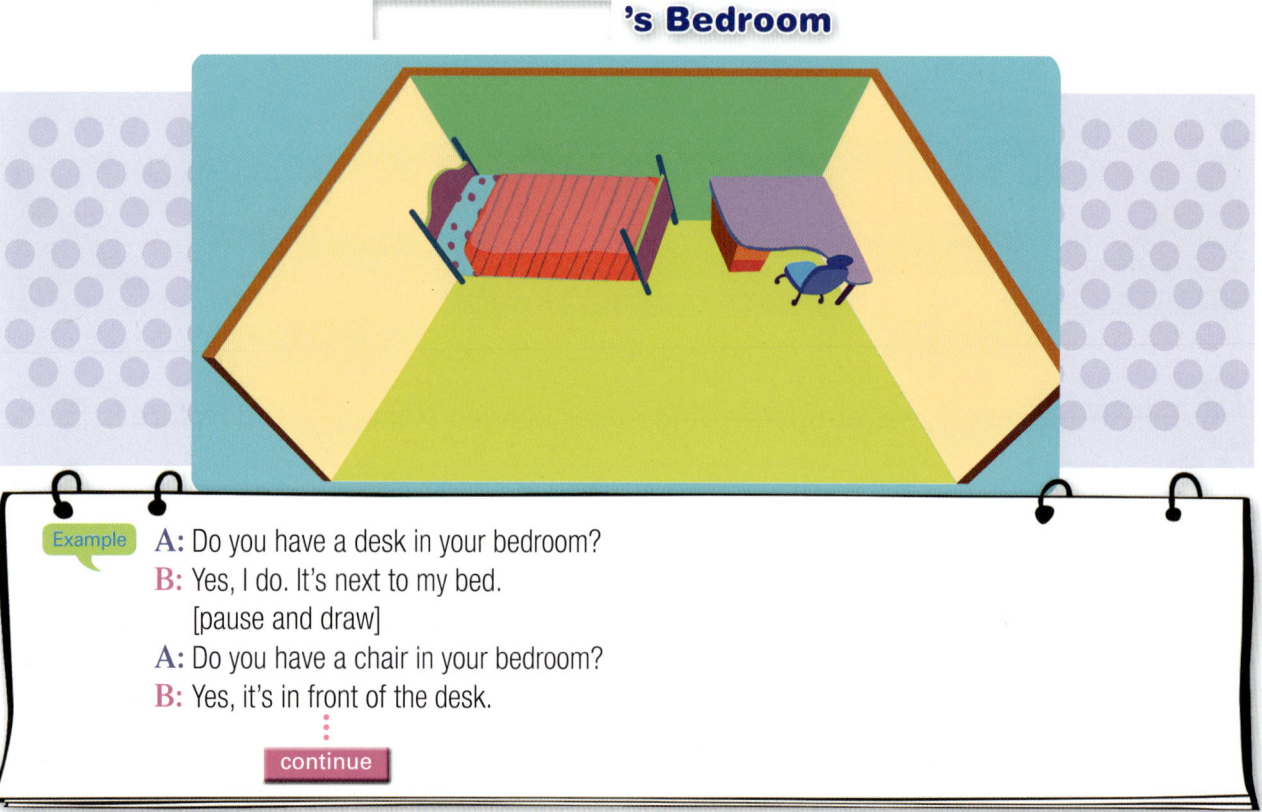

Example
A: Do you have a desk in your bedroom?
B: Yes, I do. It's next to my bed.
   [pause and draw]
A: Do you have a chair in your bedroom?
B: Yes, it's in front of the desk.

continue

 Speak & Listen

A 🎧 Listen to the dialogue. Write the items in the correct locations.

watch   glasses   wallet   keys

B Ask your partner questions about the locations of the items in the picture.

> **Example**
>
> A: Do you see the newspaper in the picture?
> B: Yes, I do.
> A: Where is it?
> B: It's on the nightstand.
>
> A: Do you see the pencils in the picture?
> B: Yes, I do.
> A: Where are they?
> B: They're on the desk.

Lesson 12: Is there a flower shop around here?

Warm-Up: Has someone ever asked you for directions?
Can you give directions from your home to the nearest bank?

Dialogue: Listen to the dialogue and practice.

Scott: Excuse me. Is there a flower shop around here?
Tiffany: Yes, there's one just around the corner.
Scott: I'm new to the area. Could you be more specific?
Tiffany: Sure, walk straight and turn left at the first corner. You'll see a big grocery store. The flower shop is right next to the grocery store. You can't miss it.
Scott: Oh, thanks. And one more question. Is there also a jewelry store nearby?
Tiffany: The jewelry store is a couple of blocks away from the flower shop.
Scott: Could you tell me how to get there?
Tiffany: Hmm ... it's hard to explain it from here. Why don't you ask someone near the flower shop? It's a lot easier to get there from the flower shop.
Scott: Oh, that's a good idea. Thanks for your help.
Tiffany: You're welcome. Have a nice day.

Language Focus

Describing Locations	
Where is the grocery store**?** **Do you know where** the grocery store **is?**	It's **on** Fifth Avenue. It's **across from** the hospital. It's **in front of** the bakery. It's **behind** the flower shop. It's **(right) next to / beside** the coffee shop. It's **between** the theater **and** the bank. It's **(just) past** the gas station.

Giving Directions	
Can you tell me how to get to the hair salon? **Could you tell me the way to** the hair salon?	**Go straight** for one block. **Walk straight** for two blocks. **Turn left** at the first corner. **Make a left turn** at the second corner. **Turn right** at the first intersection. **Make a right turn** at the second intersection. **Cross** the street.

 Pronunciation   Listen to the words and practice saying them.

- **Homonyms**
  - flower – flour
  - write – right
  - here – hear
  - meat – meet
  - see – sea
  - die – dye
  - week – weak
  - piece – peace

- **lr**
  - jewelry
  - cavalry
  - already
  - rivalry

- **rl**
  - girl
  - world
  - pearl
  - hurl

- **er (/ər/)**
  - corner
  - summer
  - partner
  - worker
  - border
  - writer
  - player
  - caller

Talk 1

A Decide if each statement is true or false, referring to the map.

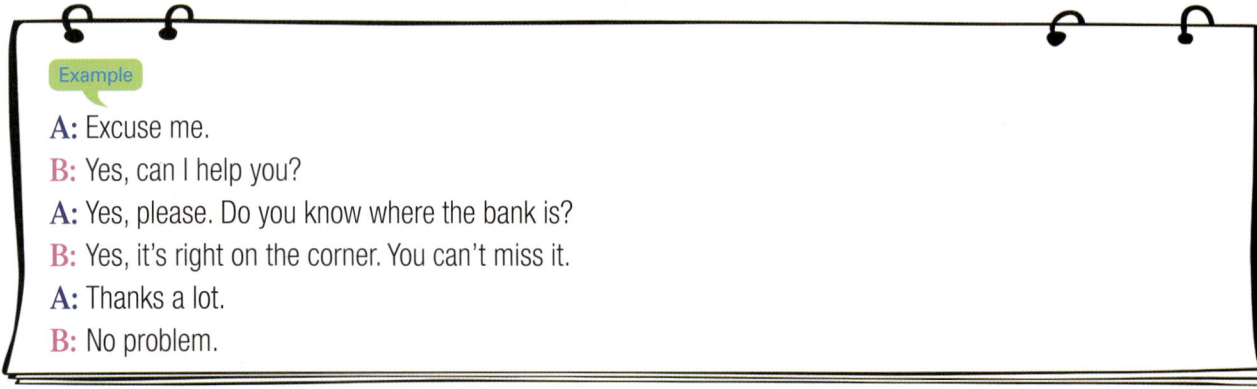

	True	False
❶ The bookstore is on the corner.	☐	☐
❷ The fire station is next to the post office.	☐	☐
❸ The library is in front of the theater.	☐	☐
❹ The newsstand is across from the bookstore.	☐	☐
❺ The stationery store is behind the police station.	☐	☐
❻ The post office is between the bank and the theater.	☐	☐
❼ The theater is just past the bookstore, in front of the library.	☐	☐

B Ask your partner about the locations of the places on the map.

> **Example**
>
> **A:** Excuse me.
> **B:** Yes, can I help you?
> **A:** Yes, please. Do you know where the bank is?
> **B:** Yes, it's right on the corner. You can't miss it.
> **A:** Thanks a lot.
> **B:** No problem.

Talk 2

A Match the words with the places on the map.

| Laundromat | Jewelry Store | Hair Salon | Gas Station |
| Stationery Store | Coffee Shop | Newsstand | Flower Shop |

B Ask your partner for directions to the places on the map.

Example

A: Is there a bakery nearby?
B: Yes, there is.
A: Could you tell me how to get there?
B: Sure. Go straight for two blocks and turn right. Walk straight and cross the street. It's past the drugstore.
A: Oh, I see. Thanks for your help.
B: You're welcome.

i Speak

A Draw a map of your neighborhood. Include your house, and six other places. Do not let your partner see your drawing.

B Ask your partner questions to draw a map of his/her neighborhood. Then check your drawing by comparing it with your partner's map in **A**.

Example

A: Is there a drugstore in your neighborhood?
B: No, there isn't.
A: Then, is there a convenience store in your neighborhood?
B: Yes, there is.
A: How do you get there from your house?
B: Go straight for one block and turn left. It's on your right.

 **Speak & Listen**

A Listen to the dialogues. Match the words with the places on the map.

How to get to ...

| Drugstore | Laundromat | Stationery Store | Sports Center |

You are here!

B Ask your partner for directions to the places on the map.

Example

A: Can you tell me how to get to the movie theater?
B: Sure. Go straight for one block and turn left. Then you'll see the movie theater on your right. It's between the convenience store and the fire station.

Lesson 13
Do you like musicals?

Warm-Up What are your likes and dislikes?
What do you like/dislike doing when you feel stressed?

Dialogue Listen to the dialogue and practice.

Nicole: So, I heard you're a web designer.
Ken: That's right.
Nicole: That sounds an interesting job. What's it like?
Ken: It's a little bit stressful. I often have to work late.
Nicole: Oh, my! Then, how do you release your stress?
Ken: I listen to rock music. I also love to go to rock concerts. They give me energy.
Nicole: Wow! I've never been to a rock concert before.
Ken: Really? Then what kind of entertainment do you like?
Nicole: I like musicals. I'm really crazy about them. Do you like musicals?
Ken: I don't like them much but I hope to go see one with you sometime.
Nicole: That's very sweet of you. I'd also like to go to a rock concert with you.
Ken: Deal! We have two more dates coming up then!

Language Focus

Questions About Likes and Dislikes

Do you like soap operas?	Yes, I do. / Yes, I like them. No, I don't. / No, I don't like them.
Do you like **to** play sports? **Do you like** play**ing** sports?	Yes, I do. Yes, I like **to** play sports. Yes, I like play**ing** sports.
	No, I don't. No I don't like **to** play sports. No, I don't like play**ing** sports.

Expressing Likes and Dislikes

How do you like action movies? What do you think about action movies?		I like them very much. I really like them. / I like them a lot. I love them. / I'm crazy about them.
		I kind of like them. They're OK. They're not bad.
		I don't like them. I don't like them much. I hate them.

Pronunciation Listen to the words and practice saying them.

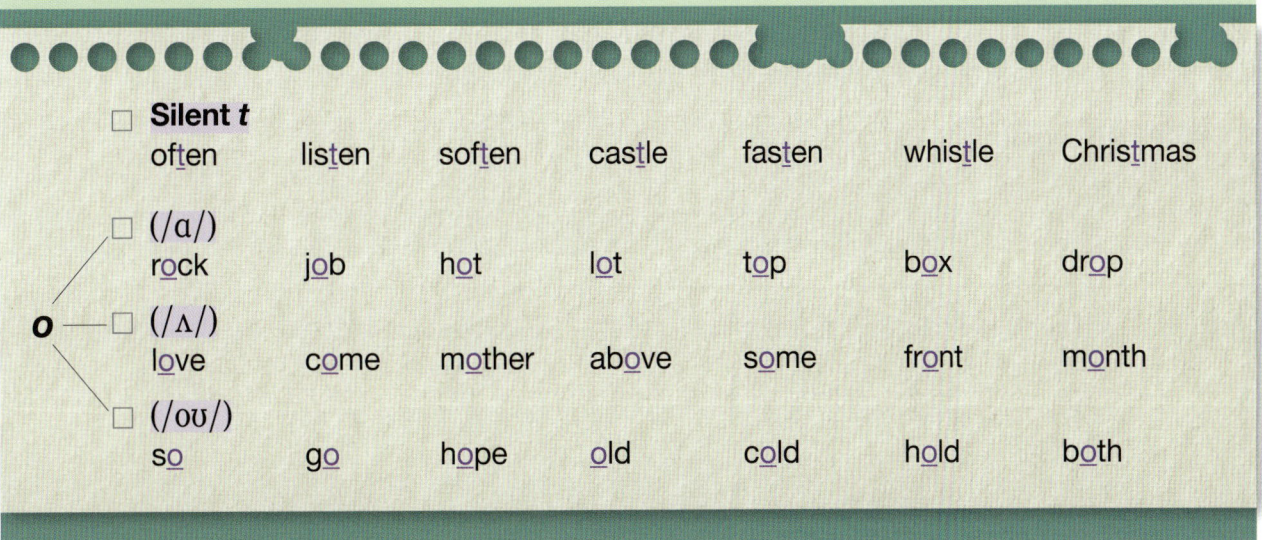

☐ **Silent _t_**						
of_t_en	lis_t_en	sof_t_en	cas_t_le	fas_t_en	whis_t_le	Chris_t_mas

o ─ ☐ (/ɑ/)
r**o**ck   j**o**b   h**o**t   l**o**t   t**o**p   b**o**x   dr**o**p

☐ (/ʌ/)
l**o**ve   c**o**me   m**o**ther   ab**o**ve   s**o**me   fr**o**nt   m**o**nth

☐ (/oʊ/)
s**o**   g**o**   h**o**pe   **o**ld   c**o**ld   h**o**ld   b**o**th

Talk 1

A Match the activities with the pictures. Then check (✓) the activities that you like.

① ~~watch movies~~   ② go hiking   ③ go fishing   ④ drive   ⑤ play tennis
⑥ go snowboarding   ⑦ listen to music   ⑧ dance   ⑨ play soccer

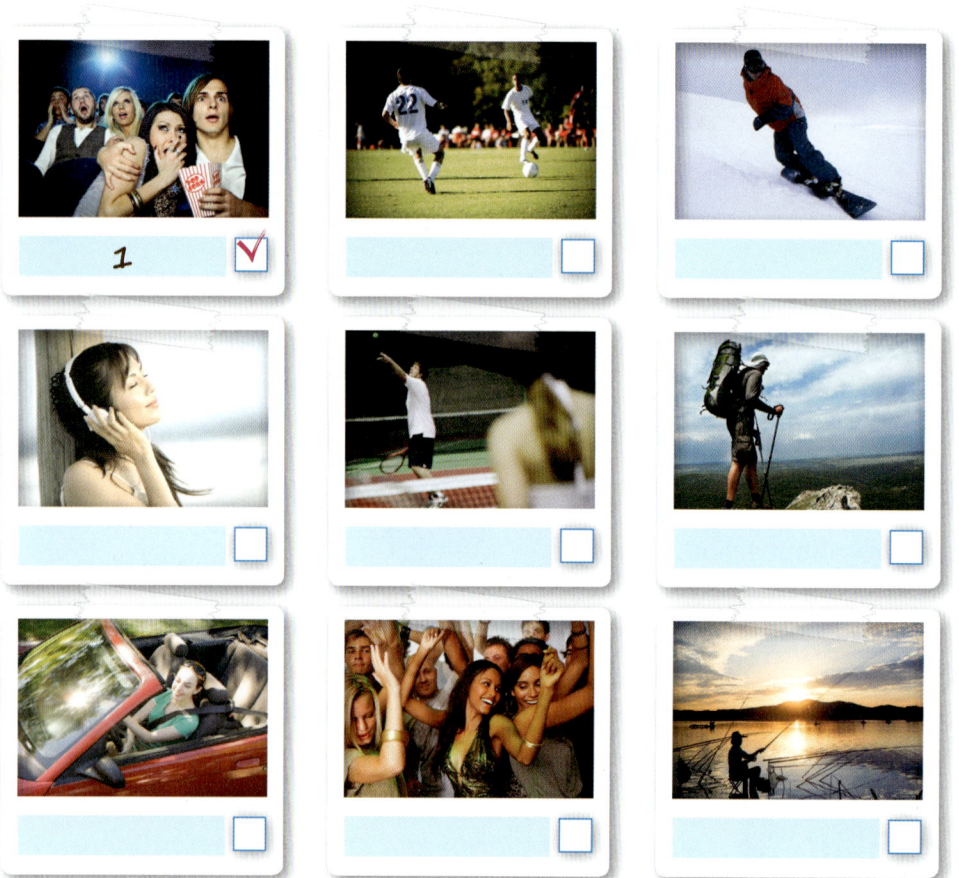

B Write the activities that you checked in **A** in the boxes. Then ask your partner questions to find out if he/she likes the same activities as you.

Your Partner	watch movies ☐	☐	☐	☐	☐

Example

A: Do you like watching / to watch movies, too?
B: Yes, I do. / Yes, I really like to.
A: Do you also like driving / to drive?
⋮
continue

A: Do you like watching / to watch movies, too?
B: No, I don't. / No, I don't like it much.
A: Then, do you like driving / to drive?
⋮
continue

Talk 2

A Match the sentences with the pictures.

I really like them.	I love them.	I hate them.
I like them.	I don't like them.	

B Practice the dialogue with a partner, using the information below.

roses   **tulips**   **watermelons**   **bananas**   **dogs**   **cats**

horror movies   **romantic movies**   **novels**   **comic books**   **cucumbers**   **carrots**

> **Example**
> **A:** What do you think about musicals?
> **B:** I really like them.
> **A:** What about concerts?
> **B:** I don't like them much.
>   ⋮
> `continue`

musicals   **concerts**

i Speak

A Check (✓) whether you like or dislike the activities.

Do you like to ... ?

		Like	Dislike
①	drive		
②	watch horror movies		
③	go window shopping		
④	study English		
⑤	shop online		
⑥	stay up late at night		
⑦	play computer games		
⑧	drink coffee on a rainy day		

B Ask your classmates questions, using the information in **A**. Try to find someone who has the same likes and dislikes as you.

> **Example**
>
> A: John, do you like driving?
> A: Do you like to watch horror movies?
> A: Oh, then I should ask someone else.
>   Sarah, do you like horror movies?
>
> B: Yes, I really like driving.
> B: No, I don't. I hate horror movies.
> C: Yes, I love them.

 Speak & Listen

A Listen to the dialogue. Complete the table below.

	Cindy	Maria	Carlos	Amy	Jeff
Likes	puppies				
Dislikes	cats				

B Listen again and write the reasons for the people's likes and dislikes.

	Reasons for Likes	Reasons for Dislikes
Cindy	cute, charming, loyal	arrogant, scary eyes
Maria		
Carlos		
Amy		
Jeff		

C Talk with your partner about the likes and dislikes of the people in A and B.

Example

A: What does Cindy like?
B: She likes puppies
A: Why does she like puppies?
B: She likes them because they are cute, charming, and loyal.
A: What does Cindy dislike?
B: She dislikes cats.
A: Why doesn't she like cats?
B: Because they are arrogant and have scary eyes.

Lesson 14
What kinds of movies do you like?

Warm-Up What is your favorite kind of movie?
Who is your favorite movie star?

 **Dialogue** Listen to the dialogue and practice.

Patrick: Do you like watching movies?
Samantha: Oh, I love watching movies.
Patrick: What kinds of movies do you like?
Samantha: I like horror movies. I especially like to watch them in dark rooms.
Patrick: I really don't understand why people watch horror movies.
Samantha: Then, what is your favorite kind of movie?
Patrick: I'm not really fond of movies, but action movies are OK.
Samantha: Oh, so you like action movies.
Patrick: Are there any kinds of movies that you don't like?
Samantha: Yeah, I hate sad movies. I don't like to cry watching movies. How about you? What kinds of movies don't you like?
Patrick: I don't like romantic comedies. They're too clichéd.

Language Focus

Questions About Likes and Dislikes	
What kinds of sports do / don't you like?	I like tennis. / I don't like tennis.
What kinds of sports do / don't you like to play?	I like to play tennis. / I don't like to play tennis.
What kinds of sports do / don't you like playing?	I like playing tennis. / I don't like playing tennis.
What's your favorite sport? What's your favorite kind of sport?	My favorite sport is tennis. My favorite kind of sport is tennis.
Who is your favorite tennis player? Who is the tennis player that you like the most?	Maria Sharapova is my favorite tennis player. I like Maria Sharapova the most.
Why do you like tennis? What's your reason for liking tennis?	It helps me to stay fit. I like tennis because it helps me (to) stay fit.

Pronunciation
Listen to the words and practice saying them.

☐ **rr**
| horror | borrow | ferry | hurry | carry |
| merry | sorry | furry | mirror | terror |

☐ **ion** (/ʃən/)
| action | passion | mission | option | caution |
| vacation | location | section | station | emotion |

☐ **Loanwords** (French → English)
| cliché | café | chef | entrée | genre |

Talk 1

A Check (✓) whether you like or dislike the activities.

You

Movies

	Like	Dislike
thrillers		
comedies		
horror movies		
action movies		
romance movies		
animated movies		
romantic comedies		

TV Programs

	Like	Dislike
news		
sitcoms		
cartoons		
talk shows		
quiz shows		
soap operas		
documentaries		

B Ask your partner questions to complete the tables.

Your Partner

Movies

	Like	Dislike
thrillers		
comedies		
horror movies		
action movies		
romance movies		
animated movies		
romantic comedies		

TV Programs

	Like	Dislike
news		
sitcoms		
cartoons		
talk shows		
quiz shows		
soap operas		
documentaries		

Example

A: What kinds of movies do you like?
B: I like comedies.
A: Why do you like comedies?
B: They make me laugh.

A: What kinds of TV programs don't you like?
B: I don't like documentaries.
A: Why don't you like documentaries?
B: I find them boring.

Talk 2

A Check (✓) the kinds of music and sports that you like. Then write your favorite artists/sportspeople for each kind of music/sport that you like.

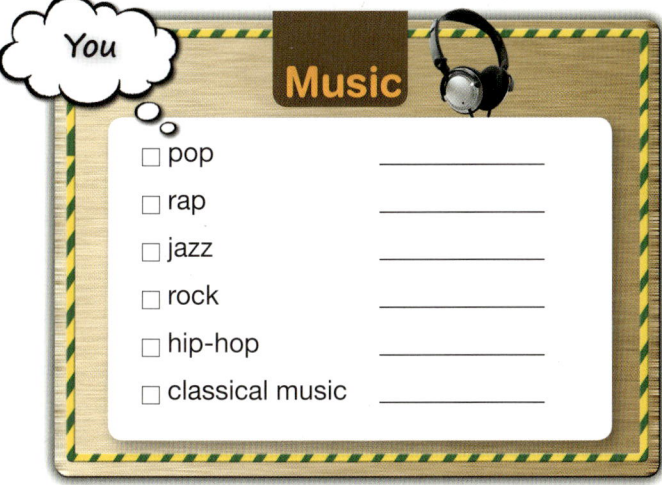

B Ask your partner questions to complete the tables.

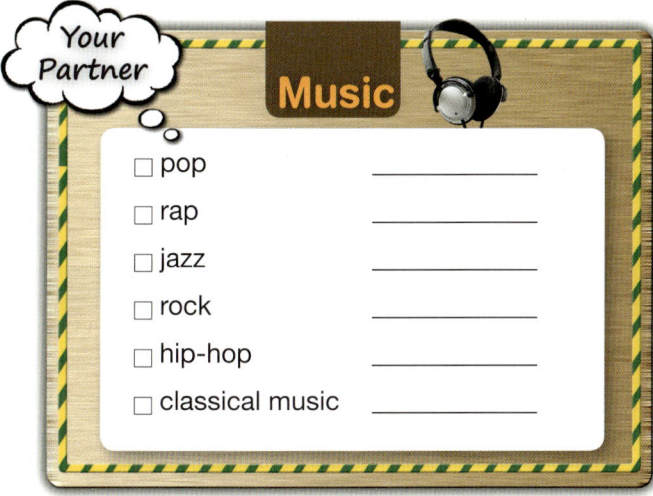

A: What's your favorite kind of music?
B: I like jazz.
A: Who's your favorite jazz artist?
B: Nora Jones is my favorite jazz artist.

A: What's your favorite sport?
B: I like basketball.
A: Who's your favorite basketball player?
B: Kobe Bryant is my favorite basketball player.

i Speak

A Ask four classmates questions to complete the survey. Add an extra category of your own.

	Name	Weather	Food	
1				
2				
3				
4				

B Tell your partner what you found out about one of your classmates.

Example

A: Who did you speak to first?
B: I spoke to Sam first.
A: What kind of weather does Sam like?
B: He loves the sun.
A: What is his favorite food?
B: His favorite food is spaghetti.
A: What else did you find out?
B: His favorite actress is Nicole Kidman.

 **Speak & Listen**

A 🎧 Listen to the dialogue. Complete the table below with what Grace, Tracy, Richard, and Tom like.

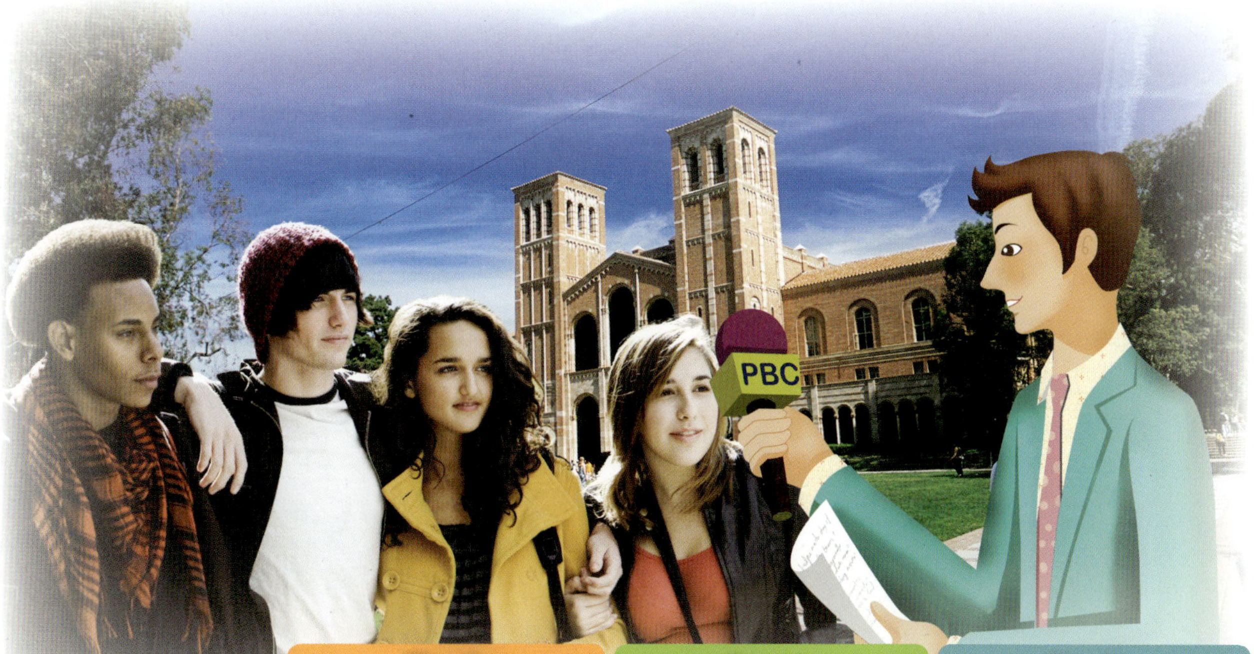

	Music	Sports	Movies
Grace			
Tracy			
Richard			
Tom			

 Talk with your partner about what the people in **A** like.

Example

A: What kind of music does Brian like?
B: He likes (to listen to) rap music.
A: What kind of sports does Brian like?
B: He likes (to play) baseball.
A: What kind of movies does Brian like?
B: He likes (to watch) action movies.

Lesson 15: I'm looking for a minidress.

Warm-Up Do you like shopping? How often do you go shopping? Where do you usually go shopping? What do you usually buy?

Dialogue Listen to the dialogue and practice.

Salesperson: Hello. Can I help you?
Grace: Yes, I'm looking for a minidress.
Salesperson: Do you have any style in mind?
Grace: Hmm … I want it to be short, but it should look classy.
Salesperson: Then, how about this one? It's a new arrival.
Grace: Oh, I love it. Does it come in black?
Salesperson: Yes, it does.
Grace: Do you have it in medium?
Salesperson: Let's see. Yes, here's a medium. Do you want to try it on?
Grace: I wish I could, but I'm in a rush right now. Can I get a refund if I buy it now and it doesn't fit?
Salesperson: I'm sorry. We don't give refunds.
Grace: Then, could I exchange it for another one if it doesn't fit?
Salesperson: Sure. That's no problem. Just bring it back within a week with the receipt.

Language Focus

Salesperson → Customer

Can I help you?	I'm looking for a jacket.
What can I do for you?	I'm just looking, thanks.

Customer → Salesperson

Do you have this in medium?	Yes, we do. / No, we don't.
Does this come in pink?	Yes, it does. / No, it doesn't.
Can I get a refund for this?	Yes, we can give you a refund.
I'd like to return this for a refund.	I'm sorry. We don't give refunds.
Can I exchange this for another one?	OK. You can exchange it.
I'd like to exchange this for another one.	I'm sorry. Exchanges are not allowed.

Pronunciation — Listen to the words and practice saying them.

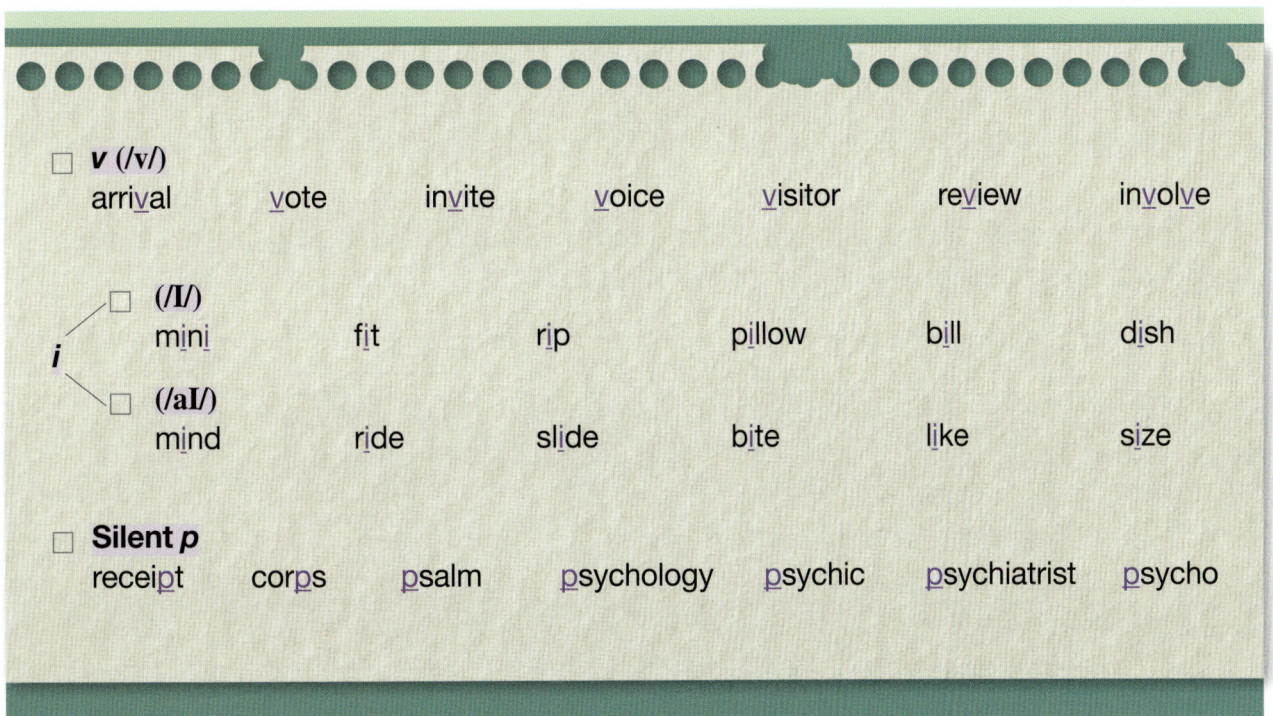

☐ **v (/v/)**
arrival   vote   invite   voice   visitor   review   involve

i
 ☐ **(/ɪ/)**
 mini   fit   rip   pillow   bill   dish

 ☐ **(/aɪ/)**
 mind   ride   slide   bite   like   size

☐ **Silent p**
receipt   corps   psalm   psychology   psychic   psychiatrist   psycho

Talk 1

A Complete the sentences, using the appropriate words from the box. Refer to the pictures.

| blouse | skirt | coat | jacket | suit | sweater |

Things to Buy:

1. navy _____ (size six)
2. yellow _____ (medium)
3. brown _____ (large)
4. green _____ (size ten)
5. gray _____ (extra large)
6. red _____ (small)

B Imagine that you are shopping at a department store. Roleplay conversations with your partner, using the information in **A**.

Example

A: Can I help you?
B: Yes, I'm looking for a dress.
A: We have a great selection of dresses. Take a look around.
B: Hmm … I like this one. Do you have it in size eight?
A: Yes, we do.
B: And does it come in pink?
A: Yes, it does. Here you are.

pink _dress_ (size eight)

Talk 2

A Complete the sentences, using the appropriate words from the box. Refer to the pictures.

| missing a button | broken | the wrong size | poorly made |

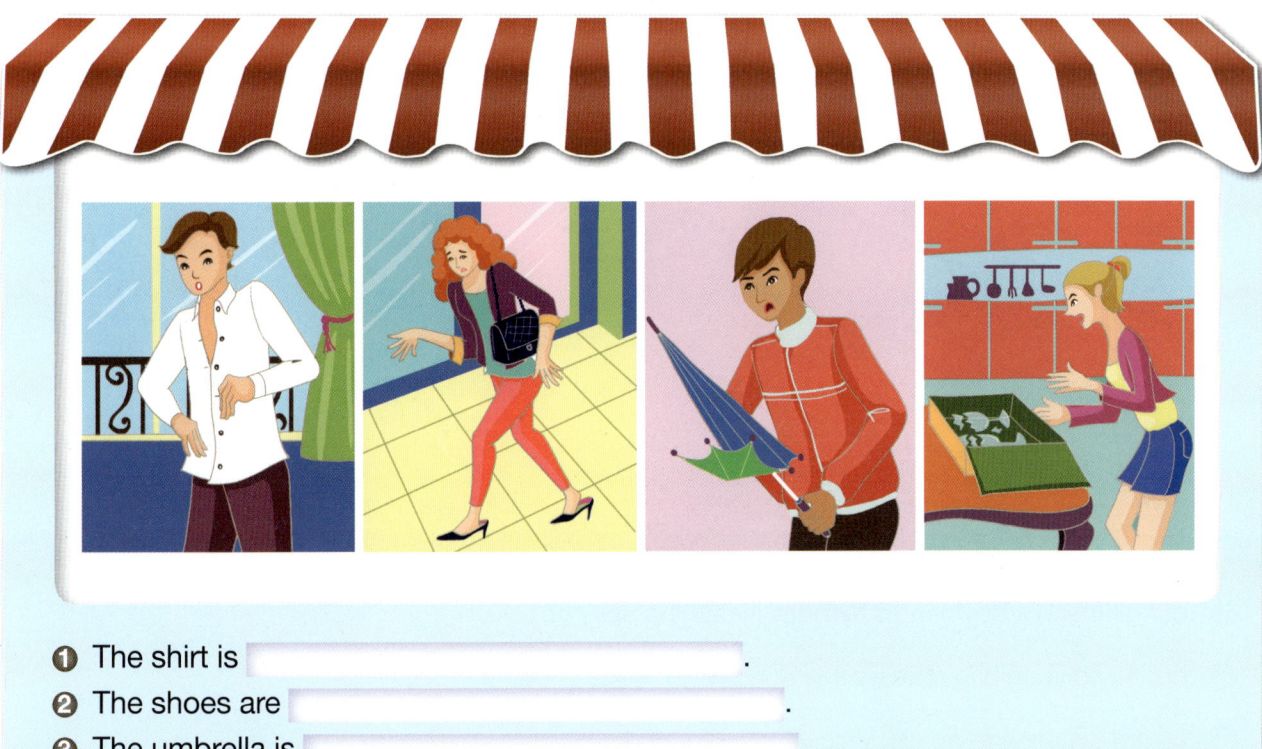

1. The shirt is _____.
2. The shoes are _____.
3. The umbrella is _____.
4. The wine glasses are _____.

B Ask your partner for a refund for the items in **A**.

Example

A: I'd like to get a refund for this blouse, please.
B: Oh, I'm sorry. We don't give refunds.
A: Then, can I exchange it for another one?
B: Sure. What's the problem with it?
A: It's too tight.
B: OK. We can exchange it for another one.
A: Thanks a lot.

The blouse is _too tight_.

i Speak

A Imagine that you are in the following situations. Complete the table with what you need to buy.

Situation	What to Buy
❶ Your girlfriend's/boyfriend's birthday is coming up.	
❷ Your friend is getting married this Sunday.	
❸ You are planning to go camping with your friends.	
❹ Your cousin is having a housewarming party this Saturday.	

B Roleplay one of the situations in **A** with your partner.

Example

A: Hi. Can I help you?
B: Yes, I'm looking for a coffee maker.
A: Do you have any particular style in mind?
B: Well, I don't know. It's for my friend. She's getting married this Sunday.
A: Then how about this black coffee maker?
B: That's nice. Do you have it in a smaller size?
A: Yes, we do. Here's one.
B: That's perfect. How much is it?
A: It's 37 dollars.
B: That's reasonable. I'll take it.

Speak & Listen

A
Listen and match dialogues 1–4 with the pictures.

B
Listen again and complete the table below.

Dialogue	Problem	Result		
		exchange	refund	other
1				
2				
3				
4				

C
Roleplay one of the situations in **A** with your partner.

Example

A: Queen's Home Shopping. What can I do for you?
B: Hi. I'd like to exchange the bag I bought.
A: May I ask what's wrong with it?
B: It's poorly made. The strap is torn.
A: Oh, I'm very sorry about that. We will exchange it for another one.
B: Thanks a lot.

Lesson 16
What's today's special?

Warm-Up Describe your favorite restaurant.
What is your favorite dish?

Dialogue Listen to the dialogue and practice.

Waiter: Are you ready to order?
Stella: Yes. What's today's special?
Waiter: It's filet mignon served with a red wine sauce.
Stella: That sounds delicious. I'll have that.
Waiter: How would you like your steak cooked?
Stella: Medium rare, please.
Waiter: All right. And would you like soup or salad with that?
Stella: I'll have the salmon salad. What kinds of dressing do you have?
Waiter: We have house, French, Italian, and thousand island.
Stella: Italian, please.
Waiter: Would you like anything to drink?
Stella: I'd like a glass of red wine.
Waiter: I'll bring it right away.

Language Focus

Taking and Placing Orders

Are you ready to order?	**Yes, I'll have** the rib-eye steak and a glass of red wine.
May I take your order?	I haven't decided yet. I'll order a little bit later.
How would you like your steak cooked?	Well done. / Medium well done. / Medium. / Medium rare. / Rare.
What's today's special? What's the chef's recommendation?	**It's** filet mignon with a mushroom sauce.
What would you like on the side?	**I'd like** mashed potatoes / a baked potato / steamed vegetables.
What kind of dressing would you like on your salad?	I'd like mine plain. I'd like house / French / Italian / thousand island (dressing).
Would you like anything to drink? What would you like to drink?	**I'd like a glass of** white wine.

Checking on Customers and Making Complaints

Is everything okay?	Yes, everything is great. This is too salty / spicy / sour / sweet. This is overcooked / undercooked.
How is your soup / dessert?	It's delicious. / It tastes great. It's OK. It tastes awful.

Pronunciation   *Listen to the words and practice saying them.*

- ☐ **sau** (/sɔː/)
  - sauce   sausage   saucer   sauna
- ☐ **Silent *l***
  - would   salmon   calm   half   calf
- ☐ ***l* vs *r***
  - glass ⟷ grass   clown ⟷ crown   glow ⟷ grow   fly ⟷ fry   clash ⟷ crash

Talk 1

A Complete the menu, using the appropriate words from the box.

| House Salad | T-Bone Steak | Mineral Water | Chocolate Sundae |
| Fruit Pie | Lemonade | Shrimp Cocktail | Grilled Chicken |

Menu

Appetizers
- Vegetable Soup
- Spicy Chicken Wings
-
-

Main Dishes
- Oriental Barbecue Ribs
- Roasted Duck with Orange Sauce
-
-

Desserts
- Cheesecake
- Ice Cream
-
-

Drinks
- Coffee / Tea
- Soda
-
-

B Imagine that you are in a restaurant. Roleplay conversations with your partner, using the information in **A**.

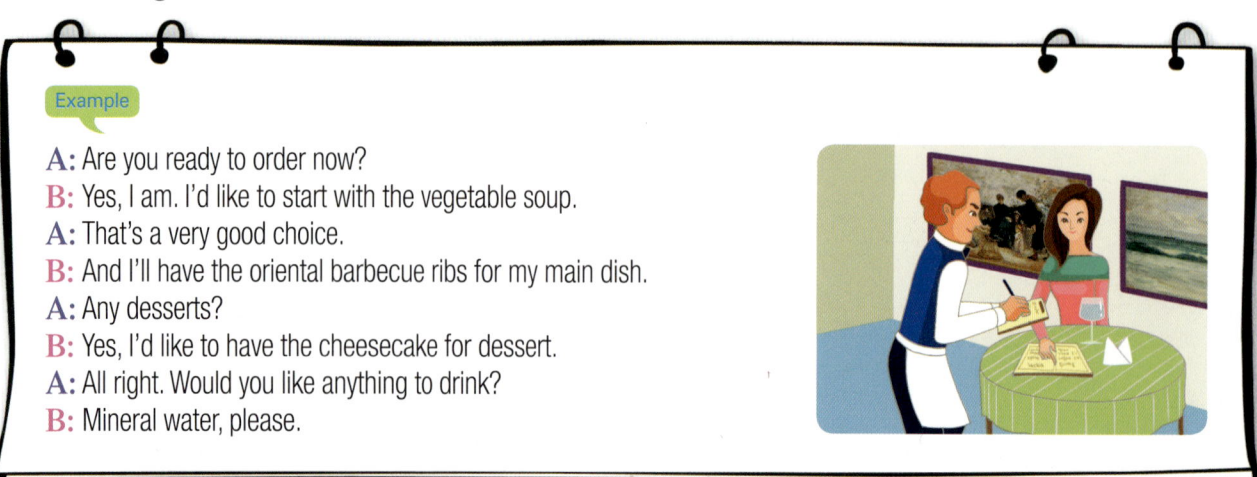

Example

A: Are you ready to order now?
B: Yes, I am. I'd like to start with the vegetable soup.
A: That's a very good choice.
B: And I'll have the oriental barbecue ribs for my main dish.
A: Any desserts?
B: Yes, I'd like to have the cheesecake for dessert.
A: All right. Would you like anything to drink?
B: Mineral water, please.

Talk 2

A Match the words with the pictures.

| overcooked | spicy | salty | undercooked | sour | sweet |

B Imagine that you are in a restaurant. Roleplay conversations with your partner, using the information in **A**.

Example

A: Is everything okay?
B: Yes, everything is great, but the soup is too salty.
A: Oh, I'm terribly sorry. I'll bring you another one right away.
B: Thank you.
A: Would you like anything else?
B: Yes, could you bring me a glass of water?
A: Certainly.

i Speak

A Make your own menu with your partner. Then circle the things that you would like to order.

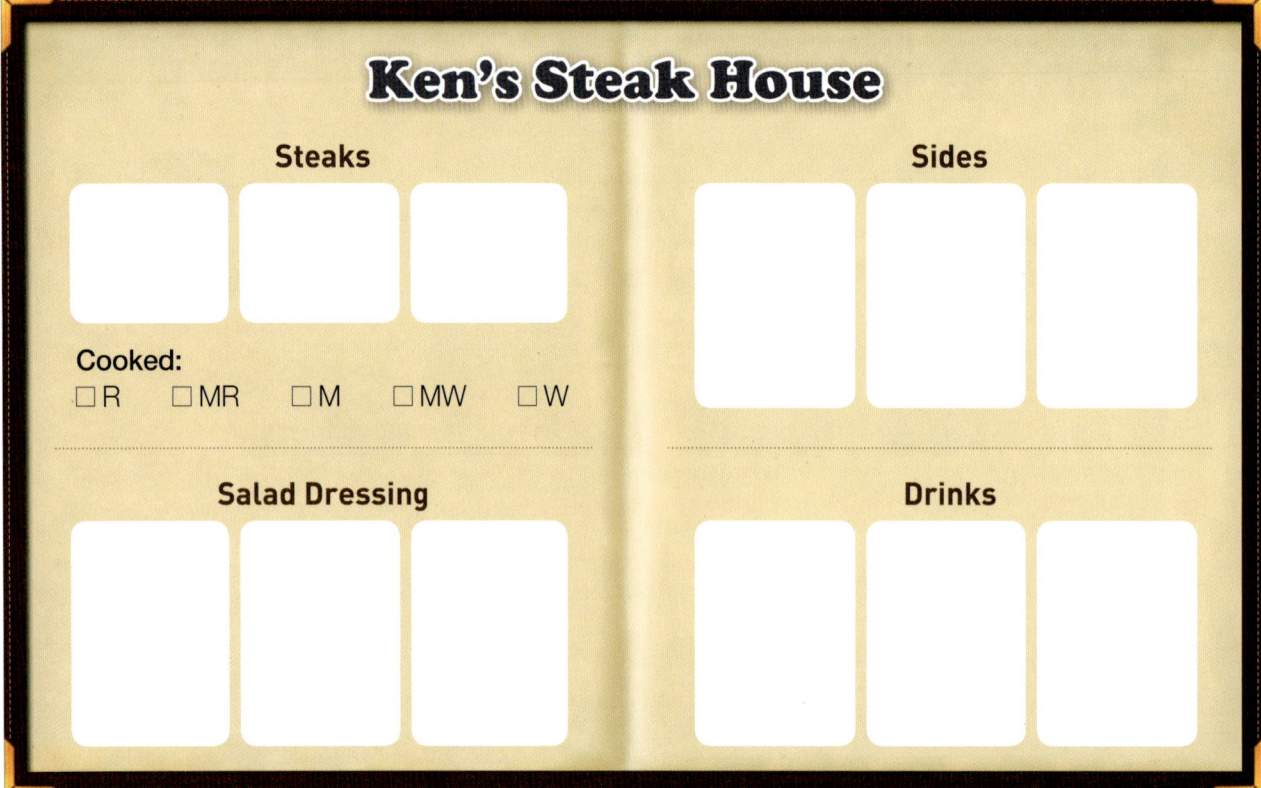

B Imagine that you are in a restaurant. Roleplay conversations with your partner, using the information in **A**.

Example

A: May I take your order?
B: Yes, I'd like to have the New York strip steak.
A: How would you like your steak?
B: Medium rare, please.
A: And what would you like on the side?
B: I'll have the baked potato with sour cream.
A: We serve the steak with house salad. What kind of dressing would you like?
B: French, please.
A: And anything to drink?
B: A glass of red wine, please.

 **Speak & Listen**

A 🎧 Listen to the dialogues. Check (✓) the foods that the customers order.

1

☐ Chicken Wings    ☐ Caesar Salad

2

☐ Lemonade    ☐ Beer

3

☐ Spicy Noodle Soup    ☐ Spicy Barbecue Chicken

4

☐ Baked Potato    ☐ Mashed Potatoes

B Imagine that you are in a restaurant. Roleplay conversations with your partner, using the information in **A**.

Example

A: What would you like to have for your side dish?
B: What do you have?
A: We have steamed vegetables and French fries.
B: I'll have the vegetables.
A: That's an excellent choice. I'll get it right away.

Lesson 16 · 103

Listening Scripts

Lesson 1

A Listen to the dialogues. Match the names with the pictures.

James: Crystal, I'd like to introduce my brother, Eric. Eric, this is my girlfriend, Crystal.
Eric: I'm glad to meet you.
Crystal: I'm glad to meet you, too.
Eric: I've heard a lot about you.

James: Nate, welcome to my school.
Nate: Oh, it's a pleasure to be here.
James: Nate, I want you to meet my teacher, Ms Lee, and my classmate, Danny. Ms Lee and Danny, this is my best friend, Nate. He's from Hawaii. He lives in Honolulu.
Ms Lee and Danny: Nice to meet you, Nate.
Nate: Nice to meet you, too, Ms Lee, and you too, Danny.

Lesson 2

A Listen to the dialogues. Match the names with the pictures.

Eric: Hey, Pamela. Long time no see.
Pamela: Eric. It's good to see you. What do you do these days?
Eric: I work at the Global Bank.
Pamela: Are you a banker?
Eric: I'm a fund manager. You're an editor, right?
Pamela: No, I'm not. I'm a doctor.

David: Excuse me, are you Vivian?
Vivian: Yes, I am.
David: My name is David. Nice to meet you.
Vivian: Nice to meet you, too.
David: What do you do for a living?
Vivian: I'm a nurse. What about you?
David: I'm a movie director.
Vivian: I see.

Brian: Cindy, do you work at an IT company?
Cindy: No, I don't. I work at a restaurant. I'm a part-time cashier.
Brian: Oh, really? That sounds fun.
Cindy: Well, it's a little bit boring. Where do you work these days, Brian?
Brian: I work at an airline company. I'm a pilot.
Cindy: How do you like your job?
Brian: It's challenging, but I like it.

Lesson 3

A Listen to the dialogue. Check the events that are on Crystal's schedule for September.

Crystal: Time flies so fast.
Tony: That's right. It's already September! What are you doing there?
Crystal: I'm writing my schedule for this month.
Tony: What plans do you have this month?
Crystal: Well, I have a dental appointment on the 2nd at 5:30 pm. And, it's my birthday on the 15th.
Tony: Really? So what time is the party?
Crystal: The party is at 2 pm. Can you come?
Tony: Sure, I can. What else is happening in September?
Crystal: On the 21st, I have my friend's baby shower at 7 pm.
Tony: Wow! You have a lot going on this month. Didn't you say you have a job interview as well?
Crystal: Oh, that's right. My job interview is on the 28th at 10 am. I hope I get the job.
Tony: You will. You're so organized!

B Listen to the dialogue again. Complete Crystal's diary for September. Then ask your partner questions to check your answers.

Lesson 4

A Listen to the world weather report. Complete the table.

Good morning! We have sunny skies today over Los Angeles. It's 30°C already. Don't forget to wear sunscreen today.
In Toronto, though, it is expected to be snowy. The temperature is -4°C. Wear gloves and snow boots. In Amsterdam, you will need an umbrella because it's rainy and the temperature is 13°C.
In Rome, stormy weather is expected today with a temperature of 18°C. You'd better wear a raincoat in that stormy weather today.
In Sydney, it's clear now. The temperature is 20°C with a light wind. Take your windbreaker just in case. Alright, that's it for today's weather report. Have a lovely day and enjoy the weather!

Lesson 5

A Listen to four people talking about their favorite seasons. Complete the table below.

1. My name is Vivian. I live in Auckland, New Zealand. My favorite season is summer. Summers here are generally hot and sunny. It also rains quite a bit during the summer. I love doing summer sports, such as swimming, windsurfing, and scuba diving. But, I don't like rafting.

2. I'm Edward from Vancouver, Canada. Winter is my favorite season. It's cold and snowy. Of course, my favorite sport is skiing. There are many nice ski resorts near my city. I also like snowboarding. I like every active winter sport, except skating, which I don't like.

3. I'm Jenny from Glasgow, Scotland. We have the most beautiful spring in the world, and so that's my favorite season. It's still cool outside, but when the skies are clear, we have beautiful, sunny days. It's very good to go mountain climbing and take photos because you can see lots of flowers. I don't like cycling because I don't know how to ride a bike.

4. My name is Noel and I live in Tokyo, Japan. I love all seasons in Tokyo, but I like autumn the best because the weather is cool and windy. However, sometimes it's humid. Going on a picnic is a very good way to enjoy nature outside of Tokyo in autumn. I love going camping or going for a drive in the countryside. The weather is good for outdoor activities, but I don't like bungee jumping because I'm scared of heights.

B Listen again and check the activities that the people like doing in their favorite seasons.

Lesson 6

A Listen and fill in Jason's family tree, using the names below.

I'm Jason. I'm an accountant. I have ten wonderful members in my family. First, Helen is my wife. She's a florist. John is my eldest son. He's a lawyer. Suzie is my daughter-in-law. John met her at his law firm. Suzie is a secretary there. They have a daughter and a son, Lilly and Sam. They are my adorable granddaughter and grandson. They are both students. Adam is my second oldest child. He's a pilot. Kate is the second youngest child. She works at the hospital. She's a nurse and her husband, Chris, works at the same hospital. He's a doctor. They got married last month. Last but not least, my youngest daughter's name is Julie. She's a math teacher at a public school. My family is a treasure to me.

B Listen again and write what each person does.

Lesson 7

A Listen to the information about James Parker. Match the names with the people, and write each person's relationship to James Parker.

Everybody knows the famous movie director, James Parker. He has three daughters: Lauren, Alison and Erin. Thanks to their dad, the three daughters are also in the spotlight.
His eldest daughter, Lauren, won the Academy Award for Best Actress this year. People say she looks like her dad, especially her eyes. She has her father's dark brown eyes.

And, his second oldest daughter, Alison, is a famous writer. She doesn't look like her dad at all, but she gets her artistic ability from him. She has a talent for writing.

James's youngest daughter, Erin, is now 20. She wants to be a singer. She resembles her mother, but she has her father's powerful voice.

B Listen again and complete the table. Then ask your partner questions to check your answers.

Lesson 8

A Listen to the dialogue. Match the names with the people.

M: Who's that girl over there?
W: Which one?
M: The girl with a tennis racket. She seems very active.
W: Oh, that's Jean. She's really a shy person. She just started her tennis lessons today.
M: How about the girl with the books over there?
W: Her name is Sue.
M: What's she like? She looks very shy.
W: Oh, no she isn't. She's very adventurous. She likes to challenge herself by trying new things. She likes to travel around new places.
M: I see. Look! Look at that guy over there. He's making fun of his friends. He seems naughty.
W: That's Rick. He's not as naughty as he seems. He's just a very humorous guy.
M: I see.
W: Do you see that guy under the tree?
M: Yes, who is he? He seems very moody sitting there alone like that.
W: That's Aaron. He looks moody today but I would say he's a thoughtful person. He cares about other people.
M: Wow! I guess first impressions are not always right!

B Listen to the dialogue again. Complete the table.

Lesson 9

A Listen to the dialogue. Check the things that Victoria does to stay healthy.

Interviewer: So, Victoria, you've been voted 'Healthiest Star of the Year'. Congratulations!
Victoria: Thank you very much. I was just lucky.
Interviewer: Well … we want to share your secrets for maintaining a fit and healthy body like yours.
Victoria: Really, there aren't any secrets. But I can tell you what I do regularly.
Interviewer: Sure, go ahead, please.
Victoria: Hmm … well, I never skip a meal and I drink 10 glasses of water every day.
Interviewer: Do you do yoga or work out at the gym?
Victoria: No, I don't do either of them. But I take a dance class at least five times a week. It's part of my work actually.
Interviewer: So, that's it? Never skip a meal, drink 10 glasses of water every day and go to dance class at least five times a week?
Victoria: Oh! I go hiking sometimes as well.
Interviewer: How often do you go hiking?
Victoria: I try to go hiking once a week.
Interviewer: I should go hiking as well. Thank you and once again, congratulations on your award!
Victoria: Thank you!

B Listen again and complete the table. Then ask your partner questions to check your answers.

Lesson 10

A Listen and match descriptions 1–6 with the pictures.

1. It is made of plastic. It has water in it. It is used for adding moisture to the air.

2. It is long and made of wood. It has cloth at the end of it. It is used for cleaning the floor.

3. It is silver and rectangular. You use it to take pictures of the things around you.

4. It is red and has a small light bulb in it. It is used for lighting dark places.

5. It is long and pointy. It has a handle. You use it to protect you against the rain.

6. It is black and rectangular. It has a long strap. It is used for carrying a laptop computer.

B **Listen again and write the uses of the items in A.**

Lesson 11

A **Listen to the dialogue. Write the items in the correct locations.**

Jeff: Lucy, what time is it?
Lucy: It's eight-fifteen.
Jeff: Oh, no! I'm late. Did you see my watch anywhere? I can't find it.
Lucy: Jeff, I can see it from here.
Jeff: Where?
Lucy: It's on the nightstand next to the newspaper.
Jeff: On the nightstand? Oh, I see it.
Jeff: What about my glasses? Where are my glasses?
Lucy: I saw you putting them on the dresser last night.
Jeff: They're not there. Oh, I found them. They're on the chair. They must have fallen off.
Lucy: Don't forget to take your wallet!
Jeff: Yeah, I'm looking for it, but I can't find it anywhere.
Lucy: Did you try looking under the bed?
Jeff: Under the bed? Ah, you're right. Here it is. Now, I only need the keys. Did you see my keys?
Lucy: Didn't you put them on the TV?
Jeff: On the TV? No, they're not there. Oh, I found them.
Lucy: Where were they?
Jeff: They were on the floor in front of the closet.

Lesson 12

A **Listen to the dialogues. Match the words with the places on the map.**

Dialogue 1
A: Excuse me. I'm new to the area. Can you tell me where the nearest drugstore is?
B: Sure. Go straight for three blocks, past the movie theater and the police station. Turn right, then you will see the drugstore on your left.
A: Thanks a lot.
B: No problem.

Dialogue 2
A: Can you tell me how to get to the laundromat?
B: Sure. Go straight for two blocks and turn left at the police station. Go past the police station. Then you'll see the laundromat on the right.
A: Got it. Thank you.
B: You're welcome.

Dialogue 3
A: Chris, do you know where the stationery store is? I have to buy some office supplies.
B: There is a stationery store near here. Hmm … go straight for one block and turn right. Go past the fire station and you'll see a stationery store on your left.
A: Oh, thanks.
B: Anytime.

Dialogue 4
A: Excuse me. Could you tell me where the sports center is?
B: Sure. Go straight for four blocks, and turn right. Then you will see it on your left. You can't miss it.
A: OK. Go straight for four blocks, and turn right. Thanks.
B: No problem.

Lesson 13

A Listen to the dialogue. Complete the table below.

Teacher: So everyone, tell us a little about yourselves. What are your likes and dislikes? Cindy, would you like to begin?

Cindy: I love puppies. They are very cute and charming. They are also very loyal to their owners. But I don't like cats that much. Cats are very arrogant. They rarely come to you even when you call their names. And they scare me sometimes with their eyes.

Teacher: What about you Maria? What are your likes and dislikes?

Maria: I love to go shopping on the weekends. I like to try things on before I buy them. That's what I don't like about online shopping. You can't try things on before you buy them, especially clothes. I had to throw away a couple of shirts I bought online because they were either too small or too big.

Teacher: Carlos, what about you?

Carlos: Well, I love winter. Winter is my favorite season. I can go skiing and snowboarding. But driving in the snow is another story. I hate driving in the snow. The roads are icy and it's very dangerous.

Teacher: How about you, Amy?

Amy: When I was a teenager, I thought classical music was for old people. But last semester I took a classical music class and now I really love it. It is beautiful and relaxes me when I'm stressed out. I don't like to listen to heavy metal. That's really loud and I can't understand what they are saying.

Teacher: And finally, Jeff.

Jeff: When I was in college, I was a night person. I hated getting up early. But now I have to wake up really early in the morning because of my work. At first, I had such a hard time but now I'm used to it. I like getting up early now because I have more time to do the things I want in the afternoon. But I still don't like to wake up early on the weekends. On the weekends, I love staying in bed late and relaxing.

B Listen again and write the reasons for the people's likes and dislikes.

Lesson 14

A Listen to the dialogue. Complete the table below with what Grace, Tracy, Richard, and Tom like.

Reporter: Thanks for speaking with me today, guys. I have to write an article on what freshmen like and don't like to do in their free time. So, let's get started. First of all, why don't we start with you? Please introduce yourself to us and tell us about your favorite music, sports, and movies.

Grace: Hi. My name is Grace. I like listening to pop music. I enjoy playing tennis. I usually play tennis on Sundays. And I love horror movies.

Reporter: Wow, horror movies! OK, how about the lady standing next to Grace? What's your name and what are your favorite things?

Tracy: Well, I'm Tracy. I love jazz. I love listening to it and playing it on my piano. I've been playing golf since I was 10. I really enjoy playing golf. And romantic comedies are my favorite movies.

Reporter: Golf? That's cool. OK, what about the gentleman next to Tracy?

Richard: Hi. I'm Richard. I really like rock music. I especially like listening to rock when I'm driving. And I'm crazy about sports. I love playing soccer and I also like hockey. I don't really like horror movies. I prefer comedies.

Reporter: Me, too. I also like comedies. Now, let's move on to the man next to Richard.

Tom: Hi. My name is Tom. I love hip-hop. Hip-hop rules! I enjoy both watching and playing basketball. It's my favorite sport. As for movies, I love action movies. Action movies are cool! Bruce Willis is my favorite actor! I love his movies!

Reporter: Oh, I'm also a big fan of Bruce Willis. Well, thank you very much for your time, everyone. I really appreciate it.

Lesson 15

A Listen and match dialogues 1–4 with the pictures.

Dialogue 1
Operator: Steven's Shoes and Purses. How may I help you?
Customer: Hi. I bought a purse through your website, but it is poorly made.
Operator: What is wrong with it?
Customer: The ribbon on the purse came off the first time I used it.
Operator: Oh, I'm sorry about that. We will give you a full refund. We're going to cancel your credit card payment right away. And we'll send a delivery person to collect the purse.
Customer: OK. Thanks a lot.

Dialogue 2
Operator: Stella's Shop. How can I help you?
Customer: Hi. I purchased a blouse from your site and received it today. When I tried it on, I found out that it's missing a button. I want to exchange it for another one.
Operator: I'm sorry that this problem has occurred. But there must be an extra button attached to the blouse. Didn't you see it?
Customer: No, I didn't. Wait a second. Let me check. (pause) Oh, I see it. There's an extra button. Then, I'll just replace the button.
Operator: We can exchange it for a new one if you want.
Customer: No, it's okay. Don't worry about it.

Dialogue 3
Operator: Urban Trends. What can I do for you?
Customer: Hi, I bought a skirt the other day and there's a problem.
Operator: Can you tell me what's wrong with it?
Customer: Yes, it's just too big for me. It's the wrong size. Can I get a refund?
Operator: I'm sorry, but we don't give refunds for clothes.
Customer: Then can I exchange it for a smaller size?
Operator: That's possible. What was the size that you wanted to order?
Customer: Size six, please.
Operator: Okay. Please send your skirt back to us and we will send you a new one in size six.
Customer: Thank you.

Dialogue 4
Operator: CVS Online Shopping. How may I help you?
Customer: Hi. I bought a pair of boots online a few days ago and I'd like to exchange them for another pair.
Operator: May I ask what the problem is?
Customer: I think the zipper on one of the boots was broken during delivery.
Operator: Oh, we're terribly sorry. Please send them back to us and we will deliver you a new pair.
Customer: Thanks for the help.
Operator: You're welcome.

B Listen again and complete the table below.

Lesson 16

A Listen to the dialogues. Check the foods that the customers order.

Dialogue 1
Waiter: Are you ready to order?
Customer: Yes, please. What appetizer would you recommend?
Waiter: I suggest the chicken wings. They are very popular in our restaurant.
Customer: Well, I'm not that hungry. Chicken wings sound too heavy. How about the Caesar salad?
Waiter: Yes. That's a very good choice. The Caesar salad is our number one bestseller.
Customer: Really? Then I'll have that, please.

Dialogue 2
Customer 1: What would you like to drink?
Customer 2: I'm driving tonight, so I can't drink beer or wine. Hmm … what should I get?
Customer 1: How about soda?
Customer 2: The doctor said I should cut down on sodas. They are not good for my health.
Customer 1: Then how about lemonade? Does that sound healthy enough?
Customer 2: Lemonade? OK, I'll try lemonade.

Dialogue 3
Customer 1: What are you having?
Customer 2: I'm not sure. I feel like something spicy today.
Customer 1: They have this spicy noodle soup.
Customer 2: Spicy noodle soup? I'm not sure …
Customer 1: Oh, you've got to try the spicy barbecue chicken. I've had it before and it was great.
Customer 2: Yes, that sounds a lot better. I think I'll have that.

Dialogue 4
Waiter: What would you like on the side?
Customer: What do you have?
Waiter: Well, we have three choices. French fries, mashed potatoes, or a baked potato.
Customer: I can't have anything fried. Hmm ... what should I have?
Waiter: I suggest mashed potatoes. They'll go well with your filet mignon.
Customer: All right, I'll have mashed potatoes with my steak.

Note

Note